IOI
FAMILY DAYS OUT

WITH THE NATIONAL TRUST 2006

A GARDEN SWEET ENCLOSED WITH WALLES STRONG
THE ARBORES AND AYLES SO PLEASANT AND SO DUFE

101
FAMILY DAYS OUT

WITH THE NATIONAL TRUST 2006

NATIONAL TRUST BOOKS

First published in Great Britain by National Trust Books
An imprint of Chrysalis Books Group

ISBN 1905400020

A CIP catalogue record for this book is available from the British Library.

Text by Katharine Norman at Words on Time
Designed by Lee-May Lim and Mark Holt

10 9 8 7 6 5 4 3 2 1

Reproduction Anorax Imaging
Printed and bound by Kyodo Printing Company Ltd, Singapore

Contents

Introduction

101 Family Days Out with the National Trust is for anyone – families, grandparents, aunts and uncles and children – who'd like to find a place to visit that will be fun and educational.

At each of our especially selected properties – historic houses, castles, gardens or beautiful stretches of coast and countryside – the whole family will be sure to find all kinds of things of interest to see and do. We had a difficult time choosing what to include in this book, because there are just so many of properties that have a lot to offer to families. There wasn't room to cram them all in here: we've chosen some of our particular favourites, and we're sure they'll be favourites of yours as well. But remember, the National Trust is always updating and expanding what it has to offer. Check our website on a regular basis, to see what is on offer in your region. Everything you need to know, from directions to volunteering is on **www.nationaltrust.org.uk.**

This book is bursting with wonderful places to go where the kids can channel their energy into romping around beautiful parklands, gazing at weird and wonderful treasures in some of the most stunning houses in the world, or having a go at discovery and nature trails. The places included here are particularly suitable for families for some of the following reasons:

- They have great facilities for families – child-friendly restaurants, baby-changing and baby carrier loans, for instance.
- The property has something that kids are going to love – perhaps a dolls' museum, or an interesting military history, or secret nooks and crannies.
- There are plenty of things to do – quizzes and trails for younger visitors, or games to play, or animals to see and perhaps meet.
- The property has frequent family events or children's activities – perhaps special walks, or craft workshops, or a chance to try something 'hands-on'.
- There are wide open spaces to walk around in or play in – wonderful parklands, or special adventure playgrounds, or intriguing mazes in the grounds.

The wonderful thing is you never know what interest you might awaken in your children – or yourself – with a visit to a National Trust property! Rare birds, insects, farm animals, statues, dolls' houses, mazes, mills, mines, children's lives in past times, life 'below stairs' ... the list is endless. Or you may all simply enjoy having an invigorating day out in the open air, making the most of the glorious countryside that the National Trust helps to care for. There's something for all the family in every region that we serve.

The National Trust Membership

The National Trust is a charity and is completely independent of government. We protect and open to the public over 300 historic houses and gardens and 49 industrial monuments and mills. But it doesn't stop there. We also look after forests, woods, fens, beaches, farmland, downs, moorland, islands, archeological remains, castles, natures, reserves, villages – for ever, for everyone.

We rely for income on membership fees, donations and legacies, as well as from funds raised from our commercial operations, like our 'world-famous' tearooms. You don't have to be a member to enjoy visiting our many properties, but join our 3.4 million members (and 43,000 volunteers) and you'll help to support the preservation of valuable and rare properties, from historic houses to ancient fenland– and what's more, you'll get into all our properties for free!

As a member you'll receive a comprehensive membership pack featuring all of the places cared for by the National Trust.

You'll have FREE entry to more than 300 houses and gardens, and information about 700 miles of coastline and almost 250,000 hectares of stunning countryside. When you like, as often as you like.

There are four annual membership categories of particular interest to families:

- Family Group (Two adults living at one address and children or grandchildren under 18. Two cards admit the named members.)
- Family One Adult (One adult and children under 18. One card covers the family.)
- Child (Individual membership for children under 13 at time of joining.)
- Young Person (Young person aged 13 to 25 at time of joining.)

The Trust also offers family joint life membership (two adults living at one address, and children or grandchildren under 18). For more information about joining the National Trust visit our web site at www.nationaltrust.org.uk (you can join online), email us at enquiries@thenationaltrust.org.uk, or call us at 0870 458 40000.

How to use this book

If you know the name of the property you want to visit, look it up in the index. Entries are listed in alphabetical order within regions. Each entry follows the same format;

Property title and key words

At a glance these indicate what you will find at each property, e.g. castle, park, etc. The key words, together with the first paragraph in each entry (which gives a very brief summary of the property and what is of particular interest), should help you to decide fairly quickly whether what's on offer grabs you.

Important information, such as the address, telephone number, prices for non-members and opening times are all included. There is more detailed information on directions in the companion to this guide, The National Trust *Handbook for Members and Visitors 2006* or on the website. This is available free to members, or for sale in National Trust shops and bookshops

Price

Prices change each year, so check the current National Trust *Handbook* or the web page for the latest details. A family ticket usually allows two adults and up to three children to visit all sections of a property (e.g. house, garden, museum, etc.) for a set price. Costs do vary considerably. If the words 'family ticket' do not appear, this probably means they are not available at that particular property (at the time this book went to press). Please note: children under 5 are free and children aged 5–16 are half price

What to see

As well as drawing attention to fabulous views and features, this section includes things to look out for of particular interest to children. They often highlight quirky things such as secret priest's holes and gruesome creatures carved into woodwork, which are not always what the place is best known for.

What to do

This gives suggestions for what children and families can do at each property – again, often including features such as grassy slopes to run down – that the adult literature will not mention. This section also includes activities especially designed for children. These take place usually, but not exclusively, in the school holidays and range from butter-making in the Tudor kitchen at Buckland Abbey to pond dipping at Wicken Fen. There is sometimes a very small extra charge for these activities which are run as part of the Trust's commitment to informal education. Contact individual properties for up-to-date details of activities.

Special events

Entries under this heading tend to include larger, on-off events such as teddy bears' picnic at Castle Ward or Apple Days at Newton's house. There will often be a charge for entry and any one event can attract thousands of families. Events are mainly held in the summer holidays but many properties run Halloween and Christmas events and Easter egg hunts. Events will, of course, change every year and those included for each entry are a taster only. Please contact individual properties for this information, or a free 'Children Welcome' pack, which includes details of all Trust family events is available on **020 8315 1111**. You can also check the Trust's website at www.nationaltrust.org.uk.

By the way...

This section includes any extra information which families may find particularly useful such as baby-changing facilities, or children's menus. It also provides some details of accessibility. Please note that this information may not be complete, and if you have questions you should contact the property concerned.

And before you go

To avoid disappointment, we recommend phoning ahead to check that a property is going to be open, or an activity is definitely on, or is not booked up – events can get very busy in the holidays especially.

And remember that events are always being organised, especially in the summer holidays, the Christmas and Easter seasons and other school breaks. Go to the website and check the property you want to visit – there's a special section for 'events', or give them a call to see what they have planned.

Symbols

Playground or play area

Picnic area

Animals. This means children can see wild or other animals while on a visit. For instance, this symbol is shown for Wimpole Home Farm. It is also included if there are significant numbers of animals such as squirrels, deer or sheep in parkland around houses, or on other parts of a property.

Quiz sheet, trail sheet or children's guide. Many properties have fun quiz sheets, trails or guidebooks especially written for children. These cost from just 25p to £2–3 at ticket points or in National Trust shops at individual properties. Some are free. They are generally written in a child-friendly style and will greatly enhance a child's experience of a property.

Café or restaurant

Children's menu. Toys in restaurant. High in restaurant. These three symbols relate to practical provision for families in the café or restaurant. Where toys are indicated, these range from Trusty colouring sheets through robust table-top toys. Bottle warming can be arranged on request. The National Trust is constantly aiming to improve in this area and most properties now offer children's menus and high chairs.

Wheelchair access. This symbol indicates that a reasonable amount of the property can be enjoyed from a wheelchair without undue difficulty. Outside, wheelchair-friendly areas are likely to be suitable for pushchairs too; for instance, where boardwalks or paths are smooth and flat. Please see opposite for restrictions on pushchairs.

Shop

Dogs on leads in park or garden. Except for guide dogs and hearing dogs, dogs are not allowed into Trust houses, restaurants and gardens. This symbol means dogs are allowed on a lead in parkland. In countryside areas it is advisable to keep your dog on a lead because of the potential danger to animals and other wildlife. Signs at the property will advise whether this is necessary.

No dogs. A few properties do not allow dogs at all.

Baby changing and feeding facilities. This symbol indicates that there are facilities for baby changing and feeding, often in a purpose-designed parent and baby room.

Front-carrying baby slings for loan. Baby back carriers cannot usually be admitted to houses because of the danger of accidental damage. This symbol indicates whether front slings are available for loan as a substitute. Babies carried in front slings are obviously very welcome.

More about your visit

Trusty the Hedgehog
Child members of the National Trust and children visiting properties are likely to come across Trusty the Hedgehog. As a costumed character, Trusty makes frequent appearances at family events where he helps inform children about the Trust's conservation work. Being a modern kind of hedgehog, he has his own website (www.trusty.org) where children can contact him by e-mail. He also stars in his own magazine, Trusty Tracks.

NT Education
As well as running a full programme of informal education and events, the Trust has a large formal education programme for all ages. For full details please contact the membership department on **020 8315 1111**, or access the Education website on www.nationaltrust.org.uk/education.

Touching!
The Trust is very sympathetic to the fact that children want to touch furniture and objects since they are bound to be excited by what they are seeing. Unfortunately, in the majority of historic houses, we must ask you to explain to children that they should not do so. Even clean hands leave marks that can damage furniture, paintings, fabrics and other items. Although this may seem sever, it is the only way we can preserve the items for the future.

Pushchairs
Please note that unlike wheelchairs, pushchairs are not generally allowed inside historic houses. This is because of the risk of accidents to babies and young children, and to protect delicate contents from being damaged unintentionally. At some properties entry of pushchairs is at the discretion of the manager, so it is worth checking. On quiet weekdays, for instance, it may be possible to bring pushchairs into a house, at least to the ground floor.

Thank you
We know that some of the restrictions necessary at properties can be difficult for families. Please be assured that they have been introduced only after much research and thought. The Trust faces major challenges in preserving houses that were not designed for large numbers of visitors, but for living in. Thank you for your understanding and acceptance of the reasons behind these measures.

National Trust contacts

National Trust Membership Department, PO Box 39, Warrington WA5 7WD
Tel: 0870 458 4000 Fax: 0870 609 0345 Minicom: 0870 240 3207
Email enquiries@thenationaltrust.org.uk for all general enquiries including membership and requests for
information. Please note that the phones are manned 9:00am–5:30pm Monday to Friday and 9:00am–4:00pm
weekends and public holidays.

Central Office
The National Trust & National Trust (Enterprises) Ltd, Heelis, Kemble Drive, Swindon, Wiltshire SN2 2NA
Tel: 01793 817400 Fax: 01793 817401

National Trust Regional Offices

Devon & Cornwall
Cornwall: Lanhydrock, Bodmin PL30 4DE Tel: 01208 74281 Fax: 01208 77887
Devon: Killerton House, Broadclyst, Exeter EX5 3LE Tel: 01392 881691 Fax: 01392 881954
Wessex (Bristol, Bath, Dorset, Gloucestershire, Somerset & Wiltshire)
Eastleigh Court, Bishopstrow, Warminster, Wiltshire BA12 9HW Tel: 01985 843600 Fax: 01985 843624
Thames & Solent (Berkshire, Buckinghamshire, Hampshire, part of Hertfordshire, Isle of Wight,
Greater London & Oxfordshire)
Hughenden Manor, High Wycombe, Buckinghamshire HP14 4LA Tel: 01494 528051 Fax: 01494 463310
South East (Sussex, Kent, Surrey)
Polesden Lacey, Dorking, Surrey RH5 6BD Tel: 01372 453401 Fax: 01372 452023
East of England (Bedfordshire, Cambridgeshire, Essex, part of Hertfordshire, Norfolk & Suffolk)
Westley Bottom, Bury St Edmunds, Suffolk IP33 3WD Tel: 01284 747500 Fax: 01284 747506
East Midlands (Derbyshire, Leicestershire, South Lincolnshire, Northamptonshire, Nottinghamshire
& Rutland)
Clumber Park Stableyard, Worksop, Nottinghamshire S80 3BE Tel: 01909 486411 Fax: 01909 486377
West Midlands (Birmingham, Herefordshire, Shropshire, Staffordshire, Warwickshire & Worcestershire)
Attingham Park, Shrewsbury, Shropshire SY4 4TP Tel: 01743 708100 Fax: 01743 708150
North West
Cumbria & Lancashire: The Hollens, Grasmere, Ambleside, Cumbria LA22 9QZ
Tel: 01539 435599 Fax: 01539 435353
Cheshire, Greater Manchester & Merseyside: Stamford Estates, 18 Market Street, Altrincham, Cheshire
WA14 1PH Tel: 0161 928 0075 Fax: 0161 929 6819
Yorkshire & North East
Yorkshire, Teeside, North Lincolnshire: Goddards, 27 Tadcaster Road, Dringhouses, York YO24 1GG
Tel: 01904 702021 Fax: 01904 771970
County Durham, Newcastle & Tyneside & Northumberland: Scots' Gap, Morpeth, Northumberland NE61 4EG
Tel: 01670 774691 Fax: 01670 774317

National Trust Office for Wales
Trinity Square, Llandudno LL30 2DE Tel: 01492 860123 Fax: 01492 860233

National Trust Office for Northern Ireland
Rowallane House, Saintfield, Ballynahinch, County Down BT24 7LH Tel: 028 9751 0721 Fax: 028 9751 1242

The National Trust for Scotland (separate organization)
Wemyss House, 28 Charlotte Square, Edinburgh EH2 4ET Tel: 0131 243 9300 www.nts.org.uk

Arlington Court

Most people bring back a few things when they go on holiday abroad, but one-time owner Rosalie Chichester just didn't know when to stop – the house is packed with fascinating objects!

Animal antics

Rosalie's three peacocks, Spangles, Sapphire and Speckles, were allowed to wander about inside the house. And the ponies and sheep you'll see are descendants of animals she introduced to the estate.

What to see

- Cabinets full of model ships, seashells, silver spoons and stuffed birds.
- In the nursery, a clockwork tortoise and a Victorian trapeze artist in a glass case (that's a model, not stuffed).
- Over 50 horse-drawn carriages – and one designed to be pulled by a dog.

What to do

- Grab the reins and 'drive' the 'please touch' carriage – the metal horse won't go far, though.
- Take a carriage ride in the 12-hectare (30-acre) grounds in summer.
- Take a peek at the Bat-Cam – see bats roosting in the roof (May–Aug).

Special events

Look out for our Carriage Driving Open Day when you can even take the reins yourself. There are also events for younger members of the family at other times, so get in touch.

By the way...

- There's a children's play area, baby-changing facilities and you can borrow a child sling. Children's menu in the Old Kitchen Tea-room.
- For those with mobility problems, there are many steps to the entrance, so ask us about the alternative entrance (near the tea-rooms). We have wheelchairs to book.

Arlington, nr Barnstaple, Devon, EX31 4LP. 01271 850296

OPENING TIMES

House, Carriage Collection
26 Mar–29 Oct 11am–5pm,
10.30am–4.30pm Mon–Fri, Sun

Gardens, Bat-Cam
26 Mar–29 Oct 10.30am–5pm
Mon–Fri, Sun

Shop/tea-room
26 Mar–29 Oct As for gardens
3 Nov–17 Dec 11am–4pm
Fri–Sun

Notes
Whole property open Sats of BH weekends; other Sats in Jul & Aug only gardens, bat-cam, shop & tea-room open. Carriage rides available most days, tel. to check. Light refreshments only 3 Nov–17 Dec. Grounds open dawn–dusk 1 Nov–Mar 2007

ADMISSION PRICES
£7, child £3.50, family £17.50, family (one adult) £10.50

Gardens & Bat-Cam
£5, child £2.50
Sats Jul & Aug (gardens & bat-cam only): £2.60, child £1.30

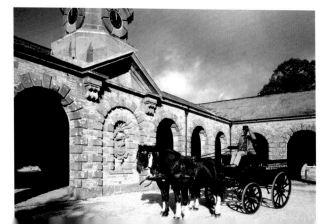

15

Avebury

Ancient monument   Museum   Walks

Nr Marlborough, Wiltshire, SN8 1RF. 01672 539250

OPENING TIMES

Stone circle
Free entry all year round.

Museum, Restaurant & Shop
Daily.
1 April–31 Oct 10am–6pm
1 Nov–31 Mar 10am–4pm

Last admission
Last admission is always
30mins before closing time.
Closes dusk if earlier.
Closed 24-26 Dec.
Restaurant may be closed for
part of Jan & Feb

ADMISSION PRICES

**Alexander Keiller Museum
inc. Barn Gallery**
£4.20, child £2.10, family £10.50,
family (one adult) £7.50, child
£1.80. Reduced rate when
arriving by public transport or
cycle. EH members free.
Picnic area by barn

Avebury's prehistoric stone circle is one of the biggest in Europe and is thought to date back to around 2800 BC. Voted the third most spiritual place in England, it is still a shrine for Druids from across the UK, who come there at the time of the summer solstice. It is also one of the 440 World Heritage Sites, along with the Taj Mahal and the Pyramids, so it's not to be missed. Soak up the wonderful atmosphere of this ancient sacred space, and find out more about the history of the stones at the nearby museum.

Megalithic mystery

For centuries it was thought many of the missing stones had been demolished or stolen, but the technological magic of geophysics recently discovered at least 15 more, buried in the ground. It's thought they may have been pushed over and hidden in the 13th or 14th centuries, when people thought they were dangerous pagan symbols.

What to see

- The massive standing stones, arranged in circles.
- The Barber Surgeon's Stone – where the remains of a medieval man with some scissors in his pocket were discovered in 1938.
- The huge ditch around the stones, dug by picks made from antlers, and shovels made from the shoulder blades of oxen.
- Archeological finds and audio-visual displays that tell the story of the stones.

What to do

- Visit the galleries of the Alexander Keiller Museum to find out how he re-erected many of the stones in the 1930s.
- Use the interactive display to help you to explore the site or stop off in the children's area to find out more about the stone circle.
- Walk up the stone-lined West Kennet Avenue to get to the stones, and imagine how it would be to live in prehistoric times.
- Visit nearby Silbury Hill, one of the largest burial mounds in England and Wales. Some think it was a monument to the mother goddess, or even an early solar observatory.

By the way...

- Dogs are allowed, as long as they are on a lead.
- There's a picnic area by the barn as well as a restaurant.
- We have baby-changing facilities and there's no problem bringing your push-chair or baby-carrier.
- The museum is accessible, but only parts of the Circle are. There's a Braille and large print guide, as well as items that can be handled. Please book if possible.

Brownsea Island
Countryside Harbour Walks Wildlife

Brownsea island is an unspoilt natural haven with a colourful history. It has been a coastguard station, a Victorian Pottery and even a daffodil farm, and was once the perfect haunt for smugglers who used to hide their booty in the castle. Now it's one of the last places where you can see red squirrels as well as many different kinds of seabirds. There are many walks on its 500 acres, some suitable for even the youngest would-be smuggler. Explore this relaxing car-free place, and admire the spectacular view across Poole harbour towards Studland and the Purbeck Hills.

Wartime disguises
During the Second World War, Brownsea Island was used as a decoy to protect the nearby towns of Poole and Bournemouth from Nazi bombing. Fires were lit on the island to confuse the pilots into thinking they had already reached their target. Today the many bomb craters on the island have become important habitats for rare wildlife.

What to see
- A variety of wildlife, including red squirrels and deer.
- Cormorants, oyster-catchers, terns, shelduck and other sea-birds, nose-diving into the sea.
- Proud peacocks strutting their stuff alongside free-ranging chickens.
- Excellent views from the cliffs, To the south-east you can see the chalk formations Old Harry Rocks – supposedly where the devil laid down for a moment. (Old Harry's wife, a smaller rock, collapsed some time ago!)
- The stretch of water between Brownsea and Furzey, known as 'Blood Alley' because it is so shallow.
- A fascinating collection of restored 19th-century carts, wagons and machinery from Brownsea Island, near the Visitor Centre.

What to do
- Take the boat to Brownsea from Poole Quay and Sandbacks (every half-hour). Services available from Bournemouth and Swanage (See local information for fares and timetables).
- Follow the Smugglers' Trail to the treasure chest, with letter clues along the way. Ideal for 6-10 year-olds, it takes around an hour, with a Smuggler's certificate and sticker at the end. Or follow the Explorers' Trail, with simple map-reading required to find letters on posts. For a longer walk, take the Historical Trail, with a walk round the island and a look at the ruins of the old pottery.
- Watch the birds on the lagoon from the public hide (designed with full wheelchair access).
- Take a picnic, or pick up a lunch box from the café.
- In the summer go for a guided walk in the nature reserve, which is not usually open to the public. Contact the Dorset Wildlife Trust warden on (01202) 709445.

Special events
There are many fun family events held throughout the year, including

Poole, Dorset
BH13 7EE. 01202 707744

OPENING TIMES
Island, Shop & Coffee Shop
Daily
25 Mar–21 Jul 10am–5pm
22 Jul–3 Sep 10am–6pm
4 Sep–30 Sep 10am–5pm
1 Oct–29 Oct 10am–4pm
Other times by appointment

ADMISSION PRICES
£4.40, child £2.00, family £11, family (one adult) £6.50. Groups £3.75, child £1.70, group visits outside normal hours £3.20

The stone commemorating Robert Baden-Powell, inscribed:

> This St[one]
> Commemo[rates]
> [the] experiment[al camp]
> [of 20] boys he[ld on this site]
> [fr]om 1-9 [August] 1907 by
> Robert Baden-Powell
> [l]ater Lord Baden-Powell
> of Gilwell
> Founder of the Scout
> and Guide Movements

daily summer and half-term holiday activities like storytelling, pottery demonstrations and special picnics or walks. The island is also home to the Brownsea Open Air Theatre, which puts on a Shakespeare play every summer, and there are also jazz and folk music events.

By the way...

- If you have small kids, we can provide a free loan of one of our eight all-terrain baby buggies to help you get around. We also have two larger buggies for older children with restricted mobility. But the rough terrain means the island is not very accessible, although on certain days there are trailer trails for disabled visitors (please contact to book).
- The castle isn't open to the public, and part of the island is a nature reserve that is open only during the summer for guided tours.
- Sorry, no dogs allowed on the island because of the wildlife.
- There's a Coffee Shop near the landing quay, as well as a sweet shop that also sells ice cream and cold drinks.

Buckland Abbey

Historic house   Walks

Set in a beautifully secluded valley, near the Tavy river, the ruins of the 13th-century abbey church point to Buckland's origins as a medieval monastery. Later the abbey was converted to a house by seafarer Sir Richard Grenville. But it's most famous as home to Grenville's arch-rival, Sir Francis Drake. In fact it's rumoured that Drake still haunts the 700-year-old building, along with his 'hell hounds'. There is much interesting memorabilia about him as well as interesting grounds to explore, including an Elizabethan garden.

Bowled over

The well-known story goes that Sir Frances Drake was enjoying a game of bowls in 1588 when news came that the Spanish Armada had sailed into view. Unperturbed, he carried on to finish his game, before going on to win the battle against the Spanish.

What to see

- The hand-crafted plasterwork ceiling in Drake's Chambers. A replacement for the original, which burnt down – believe it or not, this new one is made of yak hair plaster.
- The 'magic' drum in the Pym Gallery. It's said that if ever England is in danger you should beat the drum and Drake will come back from the dead.
- The craft workshops in the ox sheds, where you can see Tudor crafts like wood turning.
- The original monastery's chancel arch, still visible on the wall off the abbey's tower.

Yelverton, Devon, PL20 6EY
01822 853607

OPENING TIMES

House & Estate
18 Feb–19 Mar 2pm–5pm
Saturday and Sunday
25 Mar–29 Oct
10.30am–5.30pm Mon–Wed,
Fri–Sun
4 Nov–26 Nov 2pm–5pm
Saturday and Sunday
17 Feb–25 Feb 2pm–5pm
Saturday and Sunday

Shop & Restaurant
18 Feb–19 Mar 12.30–5pm
Sat and Sun
25 Mar–29 Oct 10.30am–
5.30pm Mon–Wed, Fri–Sun
3 Nov–15 Dec 12pm–4pm Fri
4 Nov–26 Nov 12.30pm–5pm
Sat and Sun
2 Dec–17 Dec 11am–5pm
Sat and Sun
17 Feb–25 Feb 12.30am–5pm
Sat and Sun

Restaurant
Restricted menu Nov to March

Last admission
45 mins before closing. At busy times there are timed tickets

ADMISSION PRICES
£7.00, child £3.50, family £17.50, family (one adult) £10.50.
Groups £5.20, child £2.60

Grounds only
£3.70, child £1.80.
Winter admission (1 Nov to 18 March): reduced price for house; grounds free

continued...   19

What to do

- Discover how to find your way on the oceans with replica Tudor navigational instruments.
- Sniff the 40 different herbs in the herb garden – many grown for medicine as well as for cooking.
- Have a go at butter-making or old-fashioned tub laundry.
- Pick up a map at reception, and follow any of four woodland walks.
- Try on traditional Tudor costumes whilst meeting Drake's servants.

Special Events

There are many special events suitable for all. Recent activities include an Elizabethan Weekend, with dancing workshops and a chance to taste authentic food, and a recreation of a Medieval encampment, complete with craft demonstrations. There are often children's activities days with games, puzzles and hands-on activities. Get in touch to find out what's on, as booking is sometimes necessary.

By the way...

- There is picnic space in the car park and also the quarry orchard.
- The normal visitor route has many steps, and the grounds are only partly accessible. Alternative routes and wheelchairs are available. There are Braille guides and touchable objects.
- Children should be accompanied by an adult for family events (and vice versa!).
- Dogs are welcome in the car park only, and only on leads. There are dog posts in the shade so your furry friend can wait in comfort.

Castle Drogo

Historic house   Garden   Walks

Situated high on a rocky outcrop above the dramatic Teign Gorge, it looks like a real medieval castle but it's actually an early 20th-century confection designed by the famous architect Edwin Lutyens. Inside it's a modern, comfortable home with a large garden to let off steam in.

Supermarket man
The first owner, Julius Drewe, became a millionaire at age 33 through his chain of grocery shops. He really wanted to have famous ancestors so he 'discovered' that he was descended from a Norman baron called Drogo de Teign – hence the name of the castle! Spot the fake castle features like arrow slits and portcullis.

What to see
* Family events programme running from March to December, with trails, re-enactments, themed weekends and something to do daily during school holidays.
* See how many lions you can see – it was the family emblem.
* Look in the Bunty House in the garden, where Julius' grandchildren used to play and the newly restored 100-year-old dolls' house.

What to do
* Walk down the servants' staircase – they had their own, so that the family wouldn't have to bump into them.
* Find the telephone and the lift, which were 'mod-cons' at that time.
* Play croquet on the lawn (hire equipment from us) and be frightfully posh.

By the way...
* There's a children's play area and we can lend you hip-carrying infant seats. Baby-changing facilites and picnic area.
* There's a children's quiz/trail and a family guide.
* Wheelchairs available and ramped entrance, but no access upstairs.

Drewsteignton, nr Exeter, Devon, EX6 6PB. 01647 433306

South West

OPENING TIMES

Castle
4 Mar–12 Mar 11am–4pm
Sat–Sun
18 Mar–29 Oct 11am–5pm
Mon, Wed–Sun
30 Oct–5 Nov 11am–4pm
Mon, Wed–Sun
9 Dec–17 Dec 12pm–4pm
Sat–Sun

Garden, Shop, Visitor Centre and Visitor tea-room
4 Mar–12 Mar 10.30am–4.30pm
Sat–Sun
18 Mar–29 Oct
10.30am–5.30pm daily
30 Oct–5 Nov 10.30am–4.30pm
Daily
6 Nov–17 Dec 11am–4pm
Fri–Sun

Castle tea-room
18 Mar–29 Oct 12pm–5pm
Mon, Wed–Sun

ADMISSION PRICES
£7, child £3.50, family £17.50, family (one adult) £10.50

Garden & grounds only
£4.50, child £2.50.
Croquet lawn normally open June–Sept; equipment hire from visitor reception

21

Corfe Castle

Ruins   Visitor Centre

The Square, Corfe Castle,
Wareham, Dorset, BH20 5EZ
01929 481294

OPENING TIMES

Castle
1 Mar–31 Mar 10am–5pm Daily
1 Apr–30 Sep 10am–6pm Daily
1 Oct–31 Oct 10am–5pm Daily
1 Nov–28 Feb 10am–4pm Daily

Shop
As for castle

Tea-room
1 Mar–31 Mar 10am–5pm Daily
1 Apr–30 Sep 10am–5.30pm
Daily
1 Oct–31 Oct 10am–5pm Daily
1 Nov–28 Feb 10am–4pm Daily
Closed 25, 26 Dec. Tea-room
closed two weeks in Jan 2006
for internal repair and
decoration, tel. for details

Notes
High winds may cause closure
of parts of grounds

ADMISSION PRICES

£5.00, child £2.50, family £12.50,
family (one adult) £7.50.
Groups £4.30, child £2.15
Paying visitors arriving by public
transport are offered a
reduction on production of a
valid bus or train ticket

A storybook ruined castle – the inspiration for Kirren Castle in Enid
Blyton's *Famous Five* books. Corfe Castle was built in the 11th
century by William the Conqueror and has a history full of violence
and murder. After years as an important stronghold, the castle was
destroyed by Parliamentarians in the later 1600s.

Wicked old John
In the 13th century King John went to great lengths to improve the
building. He built a fine hall and chapel, and buildings for his domestic
staff. But he also ordered twenty-two knights to be locked in the grisly
dungeons and starved to death – he wasn't exactly one for modern
prison methods.

What to see
- Spooky ruins and even some medieval loos.
- Murder holes in the gatehouse – solders would fling stones, boiling
  oil and other nasties through them at their enemies below.

What to do
- Pop in to the Visitor Centre to find out what Lady Bankes thought
  about those medieval loos, and which English king was the first to
  wear a dressing gown. And while you're there, play with all the
  interactive displays and exhibitions.
- Picnic in the tiny ruins of West Mill where, in Victorian times, three
  families lived.
- Follow the children's quiz and trail. Take a walk through the Purbeck
  countryside by following one of our self-guided trails.
- Walk down to the village, also called Corfe Castle, where it's thought
  football may have been invented.

Special events
Loads! Family Fun Days with treasure trails in the grounds and
storytelling. Open air cinema in the castle grounds. Children's theatre
shows and lots more. We have lots of free holiday activities that you
don't need to book for.

- Find out if the Swanage Steam Railway is open when you plan your visit – they operate a steam train service to the nearby station.
- Baby-changing facilities, children's menu. Pushchairs and back-carriers are fine, children must be accompanied in the castle.
- Please keep Rover on a lead.
- There is a fragrant medieval herb garden, many touchable areas, and a magnetic 'build a castle' display in the Visitor Centre.
- Mostly accessible, some steep slopes.

Cornish Mines & Engines

Mine   Engine   Visitor centre

Pool, nr Redruth, Cornwall
TR15 3NP
01209 315027

OPENING TIMES

Centre/shop
12 Apr–31 Oct 11am–5pm
Mon-Fri, Sun

Last admission
30mins before closing time

ADMISSION PRICES
£5.00, child £2.50, family £12.50,
family (one adult) £7.50.
Groups £4.30

Today Cornwall's landscape is dotted with disused mine shafts and engine houses, a dramatic reminder of the time when this part of England was the centre for tin, copper and china clay mining. This site gives you a chance to find out what it must have been like in the 19th century, when the great steam-powered beam engines were used for pumping water up from depths of over 500metres (1640 feet), and for winding men up and down into the mines.

Knock knock, who's there?
Maybe working down below with tapping picks and shovels, by candlelight, brought on that feeling of being watched. Cornish legends abound with tales of pixies and sprites, including the 'knockers' – invisible elfin creatures who supposedly lived in the mines. Fearing bad luck if they upset these rather pesky spirits, miners would leave them a portion of their own meal before going on with their work.

What to see
- The massive 75-cm (30-inch) working beam engine, which extends up three floors of the mine building, with huge piston rods and wheels.
- The even larger 225-cm (90-inch) engine used to pump water from the mine's murky depths (not working now).

What to do
- Visit the Industrial Discovery Centre, which provides an overview of Cornwall's mining heritage, and has a fascinating film.
- Follow the children's quiz/trail to make the visit more fun for younger visitors as well as going to many events held at the property.

By the way...
- There's a lift which takes disabled visitors up and down the engine house. The lower part of the Engine House is accessible by ramp.
- Many of the original artifacts are available to touch, and there are guides who will be happy to assist.
- Not open between November and March, except by arrangement.
- Nearby working Levant Mine & Beam Engine (Trewellard, Pendeen, nr St Just, Cornwall TR19 7SX, 01736 786156) is also NT-owned.

Dunster Castle

Castle Parkland Walks

This fantasy castle with its fairy-tale turrets and towers is largely a 19th-century recreation. Enjoy walks in the surrounding parkland and tiptoeing around the spooky dungeons.

Tall tale
In the 1870s workmen found at 2.3-metre (7-foot) skeleton in what was known as an 'oubliette' – a tiny cell in which a prisoner was locked up and left to rot. No one knows the identity of the mysterious skeleton.

What can you see?
- It's worth cricking your neck to catch a glimpse of the intricate plasterwork in the ceiling of the dining room which dates from 1681.
- Watch out in some of Dunster Castle's rooms for spooks, as they are reputedly haunted by a man in military uniform, a lady in grey and a disembodied foot!

What can you do?
- Children can poke their heads into the secret compartment (probably a priest's hole) in King Charles's bedroom. It may have connected with a escape passage to the village. Elderly people have memories of playing in the passage as children.
- Take a picnic and sit under the stunning 300-year-old oak tree after wearing everyone out with activity sheets and quizzes.

Events
Dunster hosts some great events, including Easter Egg trails, Civil War living history, Pirates Days and Halloween fun. Contact the property for more details.

Dunster, nr Minehead,
Somerset TA24 6SL
01643 821314

OPENING TIMES

Castle
18 Mar–29 Oct 11am–5pm
Mon–Wed, Sat–Sun
30 Oct–5 Nov 11am–4pm
Mon–Wed, Sat–Sun

Garden & Park
1 Jan–17 Mar 11am–4pm Daily
18 Mar–29 Oct 11am–5pm
Daily
30 Oct–31 Dec 11am–4pm
Daily

Shop
18 Mar–29 Oct
10.30am–5.30pm Daily
30 Oct–8 Jan 11am–4pm Daily
1 Feb–17 Mar 11am–4pm Daily

Notes
Open Good Friday
Garden, park and shop closed
25–26 Dec

ADMISSION PRICES
£7.50, child £3.80, family
£18.50. Groups £6.40
Garden & park only
£4.10, child £2, family £10

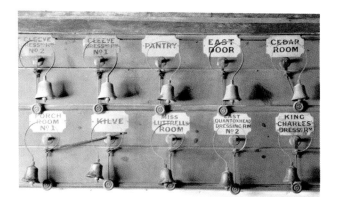

COASTING ALONG

The National Trust owns over 700 miles of coastline, ranging from windswept cliffs to sumptuous sandy beaches. We'll let this sample selection entice you – visit our web page for more full details on all our wonderful coastal sites!

If it's a traditional day at the beach you're after, **Studland Beach & Nature Reserve**, in Dorset, has three miles of sandy beaches, and safe shallow water to swim in. While you're there, take a walk along the Jurassic Coast, to **Old Harry Rocks**.

In Wales, the five miles of superb beach at **Rhossili Bay**, at the tip of the Gower Peninsula is the place to head for if you've got young children. While you're there, take a breezy cliff walk, or look out for the wooden ribs of the shipwrecked *Helvetia* at low tide. The **Lleyn Peninsula**, Pembrokeshire and **Cardigan Bay** are also wonderful Welsh coastal sites, offering dramatic cliffs, beaches and a chance to see rare birds and other wildlife.

Cornwall has some of the most stunning coastal scenery in the UK, with secluded coves, craggy cliffs and sandy beaches. **Crackington Haven** is a perfect family beach, with surfer's waves and rock pools as well as plenty of sand at low tide. It's not itself an NT site, but the cliff walks either side are, including 'High Cliff', the highest cliff in Cornwall. **Boscastle**, on the North coast, is a dramatic starting point for a coastal walk (a bit of a tough one, so maybe not for the youngest members of the family), and **Fowey** and **Kynance Cove** and **Lizard Point** are both excellent places for a day's outing with some walking and views attached. Cornwall offers a great many gorgeous cliff walks (but do keep dogs on the lead and kids away from the edge!).

The North Norfolk Coast is a bird-watcher's paradise. Enjoy the boat trip out to **Blakeney Point**, where you can get close to basking seals. Walk across the marshes at **Morston** and **Stiffkey**, or drink in the view of the sea from **Sheringham Park**, which also has some great walks and an old steam railway. Romp around at **West Runton** or Brancaster – with a trip to **Scolt Head Island** if the tides permit.

Irish coast-lovers also have a wealth of choices. Marvel at the **Giant's Causeway**, and then take a giant walk down 22.5 kilometres (14 miles) of the **North Antrim Cliff** path (or just a little walk down a bit of it!). **Portstewart Strand** – a magnificent 3-kilometre (2-mile) strand from Portstewart to the Bann estuary – is also a great place to watch birds feeding and stretch your legs.

If you fancy a boat trip, there are exciting coastal sites at the **Farne Islands**, **Brownsea Island** and **Lundy**, to name a few. But make sure you call first to see if the boats are running – it sometimes depends on the tides or weather. Or how about a wobbly walk across a rope bridge to **Carrick-a-Rede**, a rocky island in Country Antrim!

Lighthouses

There are hundreds of National Trust-owned buildings on the coast, including radar stations, roman forts and coastguard cottages. And the many lighthouses are particularly fun to explore. How about **Souter Lighthouse**, in Tyne & Wear, the world's first electric lighthouse? You can take a cliff-top walk to it, and climb up to look at the fantastic views over **Marsden Bay**.

And if lighthouses grab you, here's a few more you can try! There's **Longstore Lighthouse**, **Orford Ness**, **Beachy Head** and **The Gribbin**, for starters. And there are more at **South Foreland**, near Dover, on the **Lizard Peninsula**, on **Lundy** island and – perhaps the oldest one of all – a medieval lighthouse at **St Catherine's Oratory**, on the Isle of Wight. Check our web page for much more on maritime buildings you can visit.

So get out out to the coast and feel the wind in your hair, it's an exhilarating way for all the family to get some exercise and enjoy the beauty of the natural environment. Visit the National Trust website at **www.nationaltrust.org.uk** to find more information on all the other coastal sites that you can explore, and to download maps of coastal walks.

Finch Foundry

Mill   Museum   River walks

South West

Sticklepath, Okehampton,
Devon, EX20 2NW
01837 840046

OPENING TIMES
Foundry
25 Mar–29 Oct 11am–5pm
Mon, Wed–Sun

Tea-room/shop
As for foundry

Last admission
30 mins before closing

ADMISSION PRICES
£3.70, child £1.85

The Finch brothers set up this water-powered foundry in 1814 to make mining and agricultural tools. At one time 400 tools a day were sharpened here. Three waterwheels drove the huge tilt hammer and grindstone, which you can still see today.

It's a dog's life
Workers had to lie flat across the stone wheel to reach it with their tools for sharpening. In winter that was a rather chilly experience, so dogs were especially trained to sit on the men's legs to keep them warm!

What to see
- Three water wheels driving the huge tilt hammer and grinding stone (when working).
- An exhibition about all the different tools made here – from the Devon potato chopper to the swan neck hoe.

What to do
- Hourly demonstrations by volunteers and professional blacksmiths.
- The 'four village trail' walk that starts at the foundry.
- Explore the foundry building and garden.
- Try out the quiz and trail especially for younger members of the family.

Special events
Recent events have included an Industrial Archaeology Day, a tour of local industrial sites (transport provided) for would-be Time Team-ers. On or around Saint Clements Day – the Blacksmiths' Saints Day – we host a competition for blacksmiths from all over the country – not to be missed. Check with us to see what's on.

By the way...
- Dogs are welcome except in the tea-room and foundry during demonstrations.
- There's loads to touch, smell and hear – the crashing water, smell of the coke fire, metalwork objects.
- The Shop has a level entrance but the foundry does have a few steps.

Glendurgan Garden

Garden   Maze

This sheltered and warm sub-tropical garden was created in the 1820s, and developed by the Fox family over many years. It runs right down to the charming little village of Durgan and its sandy beach with a wealth of interesting rockpools. Everyone in the family will love the laurel maze, which looks like a serpent laid out on the grass and dates from 1833. There are also many rare and exotic plants, as well as carpets of wild flowers in the spring.

Shipping News

Alfred Fox, who started this wonderful garden, worked in the shipping industry. And his choice for the garden's location is no accident – nearby Fal estuary is a deep-water harbour that was the first port of call for ships coming back from the Americas, the Far East and Africa. Guess how the Fox family managed to import all those exotic plants and seeds!

What to see

- Giant rhubarb and the enormous tulip tree – called canoe wood by Native Americans, who could make a canoe out of a single trunk.
- If you're lucky, one of the rough-legged buzzards flying overhead.
- The reconstructed orginal cob and thatch schoolroom.
- Holy Corner – a part of the garden planted with trees and plants mentioned in the Bible, including a yew, a tree of heaven and a tree of thorns.

What to do

- Get lost in the laurel maze, but don't panic – Mums and Dads (and older children) will be able to see over the 1 metre/3 foot-high hedges.
- Swing on one of the six ropes around the enormous Giant's Stride – that's a maypole with attitude.
- Catch the ferry from Durgan beach to Helford village, or hire a boat for a trip up the Helford river.

By the way...

- Only the garden is open to the public, the house is privately occupied.
- The grounds are not very accessible to disabled people, due to steep paths, but the viewing path is, and so are the shop and café.

Mawnan Smith, nr Falmouth, Cornwall, TR11 5JZ
01326 250906

OPENING TIMES

Garden, Shop & Tea-room
11 Feb–28 Oct
10.30am–5.30pm
Tues, Wed, Thur, Fri, Sat

Last admission
1 hour before closing time.
Car park closes 5.30pm

Notes
Open BH Mons. Closed Good Fri

ADMISSION PRICES
£5, child £2.50, family £12.50, family (one adult) £7.50.
Groups £4.25.
Reduced rate when arriving by public transport or cycle

South West

South West

Broadclyst, Exeter, Devon,
EX5 3LE
01392 881345

OPENING TIMES
House and Restaurant
15 Mar–31 Jul 11am–5pm
Mon, Wed–Sun
1 Aug–31 Aug 11am–5pm Daily
1 Sep–29 Sep 11am–5.30pm
Mon, Wed–Sun
30 Sept–29 Oct 11am–5pm
Wed–Sun
9 Dec–23 Dec 2pm–4pm Daily

Park and garden
Open all year 10.30am–dusk
Daily

Shop/plants & Tea room
Check www.nationaltrust.org.uk
for up-to-date times

ADMISSION PRICES
£7.00, child £3.50, family £17.50,
family (one adult) £10.50.
Groups £5.80, child £2.90

Garden & park only
£5.30, child £2.65.
Groups £4.60, child £2.30
Reduced rate when arriving by
public transport or cycle.
Garden and park reduced rate
Nov to Feb

Killerton was built in 1778 for Acland family. After a fire in the 1920s the inside was redesigned, and it's now furnished in the style of a country house from between the two World Wars. The hillside garden is spectacular, and the huge park and woods encompasses the two villages of Broadclyst and Budlake. Perhaps the most fascinating feature is the Paulise de Bush collection of costumes – over 9000 outfits.

Mind the dragon
Near Killerton House there's an old Iron Age hill fort known as Dolbury Hill. There's meant to be a lot of treasure buried in it that's guarded by the Killerton Dragon. Supposedly the dragon flies across the valley to the mound every night – we think that might be a bit of a shaggy dragon story…

What to see
- The Victorian laundry, with mangles and irons–no 'wash and wear' clothes then!
- The Bear House, a funny little summer house that was once home to a pet Canadian black bear.
- Lots of costumes from the 18th–20th century, all on display in the house.

What to do
- Try and find the ice house in the garden.
- Visit the Discovery Centre to try various activities (limited opening, check we're open before you come), and try the quiz and trail.
- Play with Victorian toys.

Special events
We have all sorts of special days, often on Sundays. Bat-watching evenings, autumn walks and a day when our portraits 'came to life' and talked about themselves were just a few recent ones. Booking is sometimes necessary for evening events especially.

By the way…
- Doggy friends are only allowed in the park, on leads, but there is shady parking in the overflow car park.
- Lots of room to picnic in the park, and children's menus in both the restaurant and tea-room.
- A handling collection of touchable objects in the Discovery Centre.
- Quite a few steps to negotiate, but we can provide a ramp if you ask.

Lacock Abbey

Historic house Garden Museum Village

'Say Cheese'! This phrase probably wouldn't be so familiar if William Fox Talbot hadn't taken the first negative photo here in 1835. Find out more about the history of photography in the museum and visit Talbot's home, Lacock Abbey.

A true story
In the 16th century Olive Sharington jumped off the tower at Lacock Abbey because she couldn't marry the man she loved. Her skirt acted like a parachute and she floated safely down, landing on top of her loved one and knocking him out! PS Her father relented…

What to see
* In the museum, see the tiny print of the Abbey's oriel window, a copy of the first negative photograph.
* Picturesque medieval half-timbered houses in the village. Not surprisingly, Lacock has starred in TV and film productions such as *Emma*, *Harry Potter* films and *Moll Flanders*.

What to do
* Explore the Abbey with help from the children's quiz or try out the wildlife spotter quiz.
* Go round the museum with the children's trail.
* Enjoy a picnic in the field opposite the museum where there's a small play area.

Special events
Young visitors have recently enjoyed adventures with Trusty (the National Trust Hedgehog), woodland trails, Big Bug and Little Bug activities, an Easter Egg hunt, Artrageous events and family learning weekends, and a production of 'Five Children and It'.

Lacock, nr Chippenham,
Wiltshire SN15 2LG
01249 730459

OPENING TIMES

Abbey
25 Mar–29 Oct 1pm–5.30pm
Mon, Wed–Sun

Grounds/cloisters
25 Feb–29 Oct 11am–5.30pm
Daily

Museum
25 Mar–29 Oct 11am–5.30pm
Daily
4 Nov–17 Dec 11am–4pm
Sat–Sun
6 Jan–18 Feb 11am–4pm
Sat–Sun

Shop
2 Jan–24 Mar 11am–4pm Daily
25 Mar–29 Oct 10am–5.30pm
Daily
30 Oct–31 Dec 11am–4pm
Daily

ADMISSION PRICES
£7.80, child £3.90, family £20. Groups £7. Garden, cloisters & museum: £4.80, child £2.40, family £12.20. Groups £4.30

Lanhydrock

Historic house Adventure playground Park Walks

Bodmin, Cornwall, PL30 5AD
01208 265950

OPENING TIMES

House
18 Mar–30 Sep 11am–5.30 pm
Tue–Sun
1 Oct–30 Oct 11am–5pm
Tue–Sun

Garden
All year 10am–6pm Daily

Shop & plants
18 Feb–17 Mar 11am–4pm
Daily
18 Mar–30 Sep 11am–5.30pm
Daily
1 Oct 31 Oct 11am–5pm Daily

Shop only
1 Nov–24 Dec 11am–4pm Daily
27 Dec–31 Dec 11am–4pm
Daily
6 Jan–mid-Feb 11am–4pm
Sat, Sun

Last admission
30 mins before closing time

ADMISSION PRICES
£9, child £4.50, family £22.50,
family (one adult) £13.50.
Groups £7.40, child £3.70

Garden & grounds only
£5.00, child £2.50
Reduced rate when arriving by
public transport or cycle

Lanhydrock is a magnificent Victorian country house, with servants' quarters, gardens and loads of period 'Upstairs/Downstairs' atmosphere. It is set in over 360 hectares (900 acres) of woods and parklands, and there are many different footpaths and trails. An earlier house burnt down in 1881, although a 17th-century wing with a 29m/32yd-long gallery remains. The present 19th-century building featured the latest in mod cons – central heating.

Picture this
Lanhydrock and its grounds starred in the film of *Twelfth Night* with Helena Bonham-Carter. It was dressed up a bit for the film – there was a temporary grotto built from sea scallop shells, and flowers, leaves and vines were strewn about inside to make it look dreamy and romantic. We've cleared up now!

What to see
* Look for mythical beasts and Old Testament characters in the Long Gallery ceiling
* Lots of Victorian toys in the Nursery.
* A moose head and a great big fishy pike.

What to do
* Visit over 50 rooms, packed with portraits, trophies and an authentic kitchen.
* Find out about our dormouse breeding programme.
* Go mad in the adventure playground with wobbly bridge, scramble nets and animal sculptures.
* Pianists may play the piano in the Long Gallery.

Special Events

We have lots of family and holiday activities, including pond dipping, kite making and tractor rides as well as Spring Fair and other events. Get in touch to find out when they're on.

By the way...

- In spring, tiptoe through the bluebell woods. Pick up a leaflet on walks in the grounds.
- There are some stairs, but we have wheelchairs and alternative routes.
- It's quite a walk from the car park to the house, though we have a drop-off place.

Lydford Gorge

River Waterfall Walks Wildlife

South West

The Stables, Lydford Gorge,
Lydford, nr Okehampton,
Devon, EX20 4BH
01822 820320

OPENING TIMES
Open daily

Gorge
25 Mar–1 Oct 10am–5pm
2 Oct–29 Oct 10am–4pm

Waterfall only
30 Oct–31 Mar 10.30am–3pm

Tea-room
25 Mar–1 Oct 11am–5pm
2 Oct–29 Oct 11am–4pm

Shop
25 Mar–29 Oct As gorge
3 Nov–17 Dec 11am–3.30pm
Fri, Sat, Sun only.

Last admission
30mins before closing time
Please contact property for
winter opening times

ADMISSION PRICES
£5.00, child £2.50.
Family £12.50, (one parent)
£7.50 Groups £4.10, child £2.00

Lydford Gorge is a spectacular river gorge and waterfall, in a deep-cut ravine scooped out along 2.4 kilometres (1½ miles) of the River Lyd. The woodland trails follow the river as it rushes through whirlpools and crashes down in a deafening waterfall. You can't fail to be awed by the river's powerful journey, but there's also much to enjoy in the way of wildlife and woodland plants. Wear stout shoes and be prepared for a bit of a hike.

Into the ravine
During the 17th century Lydford Gorge was infamous for being the hide-out of a large family of outlaws, the Gubbins, who terrorised the neighbourhood and stole sheep from the farms of Dartmoor. In the 19th Century, when wealthy people couldn't go on the 'Grand Tour' of Europe because of the Napoleonic War, Lydford proved a good substitute tourist adventure, and has been an attraction ever since.

What to see
- Lizards, badgers, butterflies and even deer.
- Bugs and beetles, and other mini-beasts hiding under the fallen trees and logs that they call home.
- Check the leaf display at the entrance, to help you identify the different kinds of trees.
- And, of course, the thunderous White Lady waterfall, which cascades 30 metres (100 feet) – difficult to miss!

What to do
- Several short circular walks that guide you through various parts of the gorge (pick up a leaflet at the shop).
- 'Walk the plank' over the Devil's Cauldron whirlpools.
- Watch the wildlife from the hides along the Railway Trail. Perfect for pushchairs and buggies.

Special events
There's a lot going on at Lydford for all the family. Past events include sculpture and sculpture-making days, autumnal woodland walks, Fungi Forays and special storytelling and spooky trails for children, with some very spooky items hidden along the way. Some events are free with admission, but booking is essential.

By the way...
- The walking is quite arduous, so it's not ideal for anyone with heart complaints or other health issues, or for very young children.
- Dogs are welcome, if kept on a lead.
- Get more information on walks from the shop at the main entrance. There's a small shop by the waterfall as well.
- It's a good picnic spot – but please tidy up afterwards.

Overbeck's

Historic house   Museum   Garden

Visit this elegant Edwardian house and gardens to see the weird and wonderful artifacts collected by scientist and inventor Otto Overbeck, a real-life Nutty Professor. While you're there, explore the 3 hectares (7 acres) of beautiful exotic gardens and admire the stunning view over the Salcombe estuary. Or join the kids in doing the quiz and trail. The staff are friendly, and so is Fred the ghost, who you might find if you look carefully.

Don't try this one at home
One of Otto's more ambitious inventions was 'the popular rejuvenator'. It was meant to make people look young again by giving them an electric shock. You can check it out in the Overbecks Room. But we don't recommend you plug it in, however much you'd like to recapture your youth!

What to see
- Shark's teeth, a crocodile skull, bird's eggs and even hyena droppings in Overbeck's strange natural history collection.
- Ship-building tools and model boats, including one of the Phoenix, built at Salcombe in 1836.
- Dolls, dolls' houses and tin soldiers.
- Real orange trees in the conservatory, and a Japanese banana plant in the exotic gardens.

What to do
- Follow the secret clues to the secret children's room crammed with old games and toys.
- Go on a ghost hunt for Fred the friendly ghost. There's a chocolate version in the shop plus summer and Halloween ghost story events.
- Ask to hear the polyphon – a gigantic old-fashioned musical jukebox (a bit bigger than an iPod).

By the way...
- There's a special touch tray of model toys for children available on request, and a touchable collection of fossils and shells.
- A wheelchair is available, but only the ground floor is accessible. The shop and restaurant have level entrances, and most of the grounds are accessible with assistance.

Sharpitor, Salcombe, Devon, TQ8 8LW. 01548 842893

OPENING TIMES
Museum
26 Mar–16 Jul 11am–5.30pm
Mon–Fri, Sun
17 Jul–27 Aug 11am–5.30pm
Daily
28 Aug–29 Sep 11am–5.30pm
Mon–Fri, Sun
1 Oct–26 Oct 11am–4.30pm
Mon–Thur, Sun

Garden
All year 10am–6pm. Daily

Shop, Plant sales
As museum

Tea-room
As museum, 11.30am–4.15pm

Notes
Last admission 15 mins before closing. Closed Good Fri. Open Easter Sat. Garden closes dusk, if earlier

ADMISSION PRICES
£5.50, child £2.75, family £13.75, family (one adult) £8.25

Garden only
£4.50, child £2.50

Saltram House

Historic house   Parkland   Gardens

Plympton, Plymouth, Devon,
PL7 1UH. 01752 333500

OPENING TIMES

House
23 Mar–29 Sep 12pm–4.30pm
Mon–Thur, Sat, Sun
1 Oct–30 Oct 11.30am–3.30pm
Mon–Thur, Sat, Sun

Garden & gallery
23 Mar–29 Sep 11am–5pm
Mon–Thur, Sat, Sun
1 Oct–22 Dec 11am–4pm
Mon–Thur,Sat, Sun
7 Jan–29 Jan 11am–4pm
Sat, Sun
1 Feb- 28 Feb 11am–4pm
Mon–Wed, Sat, Sun

Park
All year Dawn–Dusk Daily

Park Restaurant
1 Mar–29 Oct 11am–5pm Daily
30 Oct–31 Jan 11am–4pm
Mon–Thur, Sat–Sun
3 Feb–25 Feb 11am–4pm
Sat–Sun

Shop
1 Mar–29 Oct 11am–5pm
Mon–Thur, Sat–Sun
Other times as Restaurant

Notes
Admission by timed ticket.
Open BH Mons: as above.
Closed 22 Dec to 1 Jan 07
Suns 3 April & 15 May: NT
members will be asked to make
a donation for garden entry –
proceeds to the National
Gardens Scheme

ADMISSION PRICES
£8.00, child £4.00, family £20.00,
family (one adult) £12.00

Garden only
£4.00, child £2.00

Saltram stands high above the River Plym in a rolling and wooded landscaped park. With its magnificent white exterior and grand design you could be forgiven for thinking it's the biggest wedding cake in the world. Inside it's full of opulent plasterwork and interiors designed by Robert Adams in the late 18th-century.

Sensible choice
Saltram was the film location for *Sense and Sensibility*. You may recognize it as Norland Park, the Dashwoods' home, in the film starring Emma Thompson, Kate Winslet and Hugh Grant, not to mention the dashing Alan Rickman. Sadly, they've all gone now.

What to see
- Fancy ceilings and even fancier Chinese wallpapers.
- Peek at the paintings – including some rather good ones by Sir Joshua Reynolds.
- An Orangery, and several strange little buildings in the garden.

What to do
- Imagine sitting down with the Dashwoods (or with Alan or Kate…) in that swanky dining room.
- Explore the good cycle paths and walks in the parkland.
- Visit the Art Gallery, selling local arts and crafts.

By the way…
- Baby-changing facilities and a play area available.
- Childen's menu in the licensed tea-room.
- Some stairs, but a small lift is available, and wheelchairs can be booked.

St Michael's Mount
Castle   Church   Coast

What could be more mysterious and Romantic than a medieval church and castle perched on a rocky island? At low tide you can walk over the historic causeway, or you can take a boat trip when the tide is up. The oldest buildings date from the 12th-century Benedictine priory, and the more recent castle is still lived in by the Aubyn Family who acquired the island after the Civil War.

Now that's sleep-walking
Legend has it that the mount was built by the Giant Cormoran, who had a nasty habit of stealing people's sheep for his tea. Jack, a local lad, decided to catch him out. He dug a big hole in the path from the castle, then blew on his horn to wake Cormoran up. The sleepy giant stumbled right into the pit.

What to see
- Interesting rooms from many different eras, and lots of winding corridors and nooks and crannies.
- The door to the dungeon – in the church where they found a skeleton 2.3 metres (7 feet) tall – maybe it's sleepy old Cormoran.
- A cross-bow that uses pebbles for ammunition.

What to do
- Make a wish on the wishing stone by the church steps.
- Clamber up the cobbled paths – some are quite steep, so wear your walking shoes.
- Try the quiz book (best for older children).

By the way...
- Dogs are not permitted on the beach from Easter to October, so can't come on the island during this time.
- Baby-changing facilities and children's menu in The Sail Loft Restaurant.
- Not a very accessible location we're afraid.

Marazion, nr Penzance,
Cornwall, TR17 0EF
01736 710507

South West

OPENING TIMES
Castle
26 Mar–29 Oct
10.30am–5.30pm Mon–Fri, Sun.

Shop
Mar, Apr & Oct 10am–5.pm
May–Sept inc 10.30am–5.30pm
Mon–Fri, Sun.

Restaurant
Mar, Apr &Oct 10.30–5pm
May–Sept inc 10.30am–5.30pm
Mon–Fri, Sun

Last admission
4.45 on the island. Sufficient time should be allowed for travel from the mainland. Nov to end March: open when tides and weather favourable.

ADMISSION PRICES
£6, child £3, family £15, family (one adult) £9. Groups £5.50 Garden (not NT): £3.00

Trelissick Garden

Garden   Beach   River

Feock, nr Truro, Cornwall, TR3 6QL. 01872 862090

OPENING TIMES

Garden, Shop/gallery, Restaurant
11 Feb–29 Oct
10.30am–5.30pm Daily
30 Oct–23 Dec 11am–4pm Daily
27 Dec–31 Dec 11pm–4pm Tue–Sun
5 Jan–7 Feb 07 11am–4pm Thur–Sun
9 Feb 07 11am–4pm Daily

Woodland walks
All year – Daily

ADMISSION PRICES
£5.50, child £2.75, family £13.75, family (one adult) £8.25.
Reduced rate when arriving by public transport or cycle

These famous gardens are very special, with tranquil terraces and glorious views. Wander in this peaceful, colourful environment, then pop into the shop, buy a plant or two, and have a sit down at the restaurant.

Plants with attitude
All kinds of exotic plants here, including skunk cabbage (now, guess why!), Australian tree ferns (no, they don't wear cork hats) and lichen-covered logs. Of course, we have lots of nice blossoms too.

What to see
- A babbling book weaving through the watercress beds in Namphillow Wood.
- Tiny escape ladders for hedgehogs by the cattle grids!
- Many river birds – look out for Cormorants sunning themselves to dry their wings.

What to do
- Find the Celtic Cross summerhouse – a priest would preach to the fishermen here (do you think they stopped fishing?).
- Picnic on the lawns across the bridge from the Dell – it's a lovely spot.
- Work out the time from the sundial in the parsley garden. You need to know your Roman numerals!

Special events
We have family-friendly activities all year, including Easter egg hunts and theatrical events during the holidays. Call us to find out what's on.

By the way...
- The house isn't open to the public but there is a shop, art gallery, plant sales, restaurant and café – so quite a lot!
- Pushchairs and back-carriers are fine, and we have changing facilities.
- Pick up a woodland walk leaflet – dogs can poddle along too, but only on the lead.

Ashridge Estate
Countryside   Walks   Visitor centre

About 2025 hectares (5000 acres) of woodland running along the Herts/Bucks borders in the Chiltern Hills. Take a stroll, or go for something longer – there are more than enough splendid walks to tire out even the most energetic legs. Why not bring a picnic, and scrunch around in the leaves in autumn? A great place for the whole crew to get out and about – including the family dog.

Bridge over troubled water?
The monument in the grounds was built in memory of the Duke of Bridgewater. He built the United Kingdom's first canals to get coal from his mines to Manchester–although some say he actually built his canal to take his mind off a recent romance with the Duchess of Hamilton!

What to see
* Deer and, if you're very lucky, badgers.
* Bluebells in spring and a carpet of leaves in autumn.
* Your dog having the time of his life!

What to do
* For a small fee, climb up the Monument (only 170 steps–what do you mean, 'my legs ache!')
* Go for a nature walk, leaflets are available from the shop.
* March up to the Ivanhoe Beacon by way of Steps Hill– a great view.

Special events
Contact the visitor centre to check if we have environmental workshops on. We also sometimes have easter egg trails and deer watching.

By the way...
* We have a wheelchair and a map of accessible routes in the ground, as well as PMV vehicles (you need to book).
* The shop and visitor centre are fully accessible.
* Great place for picnics.

Visitor Centre, Moneybury Hill, Ringshall, Berkhamsted, Hertfordshire, HP4 1LX
01442 851227

OPENING TIMES
Estate
All year Daily
Visitor Centre
18 Mar–10 Dec 12pm–5pm Daily
Monument
18 Mar–29 Oct 12pm–5pm Sat, Sun
Shop
As for centre
Tea-room
18 Mar–10 Dec 12pm–5pm Tue–Sun
6 Jan–11 Mar 07 12pm–5pm Sat–Sun
Notes
Open BH Mons and Good Fri 12pm–5pm. Monument also Mon–Fri by arrangement, weather permitting. Shop closes dusk if earlier than 5pm

ADMISSION PRICES
Monument: £1.30, child 60p
Countryside
Donations welcome
Riding permits
From riding warden, tel. for details

Bateman's

Historic house   Garden   Water-mill

Burwash, Etchingham, East
Sussex, TN19 7DS
01435 882302

OPENING TIMES

House
18 Mar–29 Oct 11am–5pm
Mon–Wed, Sat, Sun

Garden
4 Mar–12 Mar 11am–4pm
Sat, Sun
18 Mar–29 Oct 11am–5pm
Mon–Wed, Sat, Sun
1 Nov–22 Dec 11pm–4pm
Wed–Sun

Tea-room
As for garden

Shop
4 Mar–12 Mar 11am–4pm
Sat, Sun
18 Mar–29 Oct 11am–5.30pm
Mon–Wed, Sat, Sun
1 Nov–22 Dec 11am–4pm
Wed–Sun

Last admission
30mins before closing time.
Open Good Fri: 11am–5pm

ADMISSION PRICES

£6.20, child £3.10, family £15.50.
Groups £5.20, child £2.60
Free entry to garden in Nov &
Dec

Did you like the film *The Jungle Book?* You'll be interested in this Jacobean house, home of Rudyard Kipling, who wrote the book it's based on. It's been arranged just as it was when he left, with his pipe in the ashtray and his pen awaiting new stories. Even his 1928 Rolls-Royce Phantom is outside waiting to rev up.

Why why?
Kipling's elder daughter was called 'Elsie Why?' by the family because she was always asking questions. Do you know anyone like that?!

What to see
- The original illustrations for *The Jungle Book,* drawn by Kipling's father.
- Oriental rugs and artifacts, brought home by Kipling.
- Find a sundial in the garden.

What to do
- Visit the water-mill, which generated electricity for the whole house. And we grind corn there most Wednesdays and Saturday, at 2pm.
- Walk round the pond designed by Kipling to be shallow so that children could fall in safely (don't try it!).
- Hunt out the Kipling family initials, carved into the porch one rainy afternoon.

Special Events
Recently we've had folk music and country dance in the farmyard,
drawing workshops and engraving demonstrations. Usually the cost is
included in admission, and there's something going on most Sunday
afternoons, from family fun days to storytelling.

By the way...
- We have a dog crèche where you can leave the pooch, and a picnic
  area near the car park.
- You can book a wheelchair, but there are some steps.
- There are many interesting objects in the house that you can touch
  (please ask).

Bodiam Castle

Castle   Moat   Parkland

Bodiam, nr Robertsbridge, East
Sussex, TN32 5UA
01580 830436

OPENING TIMES
Castle
11 Feb–31 Oct 10am–6pm
Daily
4 Nov–23 Dec 10am–4pm
Sat, Sun
6 Jan–9 Feb 07 10am–4pm
Sat, Sun
10 Feb–28 Feb 10am–6pm
Daily

Shop, Tea-room
11 Feb–31 Oct 10am–5pm
Daily
1 Nov–23 Dec 10am–4pm
Wed–Sun
6 Jan–9 Feb 07 10am–4pm
Sat, Sun
10 Feb–28 Feb 07 10am–5pm
Daily

Last admission
1hr before closing. Castle
closes dusk if earlier than
stated. Closed 24 Dec–6 Jan

ADMISSION PRICES
£4.60, child £2.30, family £11.50.
Groups £3.90, child £1.95

A real 14th-century castle – with turrets, moat and all – situated by the River Rother in East Sussex. There are medieval battlements and ramparts galore, and spiral staircases to explore. One of the most famous and atmospheric places in Britain, Bodiam will leave a lasting impression on all the family.

My other house is a … castle
In 1385 Sir Edward Dalyngrygge was given permission to fortify his house against the invasion of France. But he decided to build a castle near his house instead. That's some extension…

What to see
- Four cylindrical towers at each corner, and four rectangular ones in between.
- Murder holes in the roof of the gatehouse, from which people dropped boiling water on the unsuspecting enemy.
- A Second World War pill box – where more recent soldiers lay in wait.

What to do
- In the education room, try on armour just like the Bodiam soldiers wore – we have adult-sized ones too. But check first to see if we're open.
- Walk the battlements and look out for the enemy soldiers.
- Quack back at the ducks on the pond.

Special events
We often have family and children's activities, including medieval weekends. Steam trains run on The Kent & East Sussex Railway right up to Bodiam, in season (not NT).

By the way...
- Dogs in the grounds are fine, but please keep your best friend on a lead.
- Pushchairs are admitted, and we have baby-changing facilities.
- Special menus in the Tea-room, including dairy-free.
- Stairs to upper floors, and the grounds can be muddy.

Box Hill

South & South East

The Old Fort, Box Hill Road,
Box Hill, Tadworth, Surrey,
KT20 7LB. 01306 885502

OPENING TIMES
All year – Daily

Servery, Shop
All year 11am–5pm Daily

Notes
Shop, information centre &
servery closed 25, 26 Dec &
1 Jan; close dusk if earlier than
5pm; close later than 5pm in
summer, weather permitting

ADMISSION PRICES
Countryside free

You can't beat flying a kite up here on a billowy day, with gorgeous views over the South Downs and tons of fresh air. Bring a picnic and let the dog off (except where there are sheep), and admire this outstanding area of woodland and chalk downland. Hop up to the top for a peek at a fort dating from the 1890s.

Boxed in?
Box Hill got its name from the box tree, which has grown here since at least the 16th century. Unfortunately it does pong a bit if you sniff it – some say it's a bit like tomcats. On a more savoury note – it was here that Jane Austen set the ill-fated picnic in her novel *Emma*.

What to see
- Tons of wildlife, including butterflies, tawny owls and kestrels. Look for the tracks of badgers and foxes, and you might see some if you're lucky.
- See if you can spot tiny bee orchids or wild strawberry plants in June and July.
- Or scrunch around in autumn leaves later on in the year.

What to do
- Stretch your legs walking through beautiful woods, or kicking a ball around.
- Visit our info centre at the summit and see natural exhibits like a badger's skull or a birds' nest.

By the way...
- South scarp is very steep. If you have mobility problems, try the accessible paths along the North Downs Way.
- The Servery in the East car park has snacks and drinks, but isn't a full restaurant.
- We have baby-changing facilities; push-chairs are fine here, too.

Claremont Landscape Garden

Gardens   Lake   Amphitheatre

These elegant gardens were begun in around 1715 and there are so many interesting features to explore in its 20 hectares (50 acres). There's a lovely serpentine lake, and island with a pavilion on it, a grotto, and an amphitheatre in the grass.

Gardeners' world
Some of the country's greatest gardeners had a say in designing Claremont – fortunately not all at the same time. Sir John Vanbrugh, Charles Bridgeman and 'Capability' Brown, to name a few.

What to see
- Lots of ducks near the lake – conveniently close to the car park.
- The grass amphitheatre – a kind of outdoor auditorium. Try sitting down up at the top and getting someone to talk at you from the bottom. Open air concerts are held here in summer; tel. for details.

What to do
- Have a picnic, or grab a cuppa in the tea-room.
- Go for a ramble – there are children's trails – and the lake one is suitable for buggies.

By the way...
- Dogs need to be on a lead, and can visit only between Nov and the end of March at the moment.
- The garden sometimes closes to visitors in July, while it is prepared for our Open Air Concerts in the summer.
- There are some steep slopes but we have an accessible route.
- There are baby-changing facilities, and push-chairs are fine too.

Portsmouth Road, Esher,
Surrey, KT10 9JG
01372 467806

OPENING TIMES
Garden
1 Apr–31 Oct 10am–6pm
Mon–Fri
1 Nov–31 Mar 07 10am–5pm
Tue–Sun

Shop, Tea-room
1 Apr–17 Dec 11am–5pm
Wed–Sun
13 Jan–31 Mar 11am–5pm
Fri–Sun

Notes
Open 1 Jan 10am–4pm. Late night opening Sats 3, 10, 17, 24 June until 9; Nov to end March closes at sunset. Closed 25 Dec; and closes on major event days in July and Mon after. Tel. for details. Belvedere Tower open first weekend each month April to Oct.
Shop and tea-room close dusk if earlier than 5pm, and may close early in bad weather

ADMISSION PRICES
£5.00, child £2.50, family £12.50. Groups £4.20, child £2.10. £1 tea-room voucher given if arriving by public transport (please present valid ticket) or cycle

45

Claydon House

Historic house   Museum   Park   Lake

South & South East

Florence Nightingale was once a regular visitor to this charming Georgian country house, home of the Verney family, and you can see mementoes of her visits. There are also fascinating associations with the Civil and Crimean Wars, including letters from Florrie written during the period. And inside there's some fancy Chinese décor.

Middle Claydon, nr Buckingham, Buckinghamshire, MK18 2EY. 01296 730349

OPENING TIMES

House & Grounds
25 Mar–29 Oct 1pm–5pm
Mon–Wed, Sat, Sun

Secondhand bookshop
1pm–5pm. Leaflets available in French, German and Spanish. Pottery (not NT), open as house (separate admission charge)

ADMISSION PRICES
£5.50, child £2.70, family £13.00

Garden
Only £2.50

You've gotta hand it to him...
A rather gruesome tale, this. Apparently Sir Edmund Verney, the first owner, was King Charles I's standard-bearer. At the battle of Edgehill in 1642, his hand was chopped off by the Roundheads so that they could grab the flag. The rest of his body was never found – some say he's still hanging around in the house, hoping his hand will turn up.

What to see
- Florrie's Lorry – the name given to the famous carriage used by Florence Nightingale in the Crimean War.
- Carvings of oriental birds and scaly monsters, and the phoenix in the Verney coat of arms – Harry Potter would be at home here!
- A massive 19th-century gamelan – a set of oriental gongs – in the museum.

What to do
- Take a tour of the museum with the children's quiz.
- Wander around in the unspoilt countryside outside, and maybe get a picnic hamper from the restaurant.
- Have a peek inside All Saints' Church, in the grounds.

By the way...
- Baby-changing facilities and family-friendly guides and quizzes.
- A children's menu in the Carriage House Restaurant (not NT). Opening hours same as house.
- There's a handling collection of objects to touch and feel.
- Wheelchairs are available – please book – and you get in for half-price if you can't make the stairs to the upper floors (it's only fair!).

Dapdune Wharf & River Wey

Old barge   Exhibition   River

Back in 1653 the Wey was one of the first rivers to be made navigable and today, with its barges and riverways, it's a great place for a family adventure. You can clamber aboard *Reliance,* a restored barge, at Dapdune Wharf in Guildford, and boat trips are also available. If you'd rather stay on solid ground, there are some nice circular walks on the tow paths.

Beats the train?
The waterway along the Wey linked Guildford to Weybridge, and is over 24 kilometres (15 miles) long. Back in those days, getting from A to B involved barging upriver, often with a horse to pull from the tow path.

What to see
- The inside of the big old barge, *Reliance.*
- Lots of wildlife on the towpath, including kingfishers and water voles.
- Don't miss our award-winning visitor centre.

What to do
- Guide a model barge through the lock in our interactive model.
- Take a 40-minute river bus trip on the *Dapdune Belle* (extra charge).
- Go fishing – get a permit from the Environment Agency or one of the angling clubs.

By the way...
- Nearly everything is accessible, maybe with a bit of help from a friend.
- There's a little shop and tea-room at Dapdune Wharf, and some nice riverside picnic areas.
- Please keep doggy on a lead around the wharf.

Navigations Office and Dapdune Wharf, Wharf Road, Guildford, Surrey, GU1 4RR
01483 561389

OPENING TIMES
Wharf
25 Mar–29 Oct 11am–5pm
Mon, Thur–Sun

Notes
(NB the shop and tea-rooms are volunteer-run, not NT)
River trips 11am–5pm (conditions permitting). Access to towpath during daylight hours all year

BACK TO NATURE

The National Trust protects many areas that are official Nature Reserves or National Nature Reserves. These areas need special protection because many of the species and creatures in them are endangered by development and pollution. Visiting our nature reserves can give your family a wonderful insight into how humans and nature need to co-exist. And besides, these beautiful areas are such wonderful places to enjoy at any time of year – take your binoculars, put on your walking shoes or wellies and get back to nature!

As old as the hills (or fens...)

Many nature reserves are the last remnants of lands that have been nearly lost to development and the spread of human habitation. **Ulverscroft**, in Leicestershire, is part of an ancient forest with a beautiful bluebell season. **Wicken Fen** in Cambridgeshire is an ancient area of fenland with wild ponies, rare butterflies and, if you're lucky, a sighting of an otter or two. **Crom Estate** is an area with tranquil islands, woodland and rare pine martens – one of the Trust's most important reserves. There are little pockets of ancient woodland all over, like **Curbridge** in Hampshire, often within the parklands of the many historic houses owned by the Trust. Visiting these magical places reminds us of what we've lost and need to preserve.

Coastal beauty

Murlough National Nature Reserve, near Newcastle, was Ireland's first national nature reserve, and offers some lovely boarded walkways to the dunes. **Orford Ness** in Suffolk is a National Nature Reserve on the wild and remote extremity of eastern England. This fascinating saltmarsh area also has an interesting military history to explore, once having been an important radar site.

At **Blakeney Point** in Norfolk, you can enjoy an undeveloped coastal area that's noted for its colonies of breeding terns and migrant birds. You can also get a close-up look at seals, both common and grey. **Studland Beach & Nature Reserve** in Dorset is noted for its sandy beaches, but you may also sight seabirds diving into the waves, deer in the dunes and even lizards and snakes. You can take a peek at rare birds from the bird hides at Little Sea or learn more from the Visitor Centre. Quite a few nature reserves have bird hides, like those at **Malham Tarn Estate** in North Yorkshire.

If sea birds, including puffins, take your fancy, you can get close to them at **Farne Islands** in Northumberland and enjoy a bracing boat trip there and back. But wear a hat – our terns are not fussy about who they poop on!

Nearer than you think

Not all nature reserves are in areas of wild or remote countryside – far from it. Many are an oasis of unspoilt natural habitat near to

cities and other urban places. **Leigh Woods** near Bristol is a National Nature Reserve that has access for buggies and wheelchairs, and **Hatfield Forest** is a rare surviving example of a medieval hunting forest in Essex, not that far from London.

And some nature reserves are small, but no less exciting or important. How about **Boarstall Duck Decoy** in Buckinghamshire, a rare survival of a 17th-century decoy beside a lake (complete with trained dog to get the ducks!).

Rare treasures

Today there are only around 160,000 red squirrels in Britain – not that many in the grand scheme of things. The National Trust has four sites that are a haven for these busy little bushy-tailed creatures – **Brownsea Island** in Dorset, **Formby** in Merseyside, Wallington in Northumberland and the **Isle of Wight**. Look out for our guided walks and special events when we celebrate 'Red Squirrel Week' each year in September.

While squirrels are cute little animals, the special natural places that the Trust cares for are home to so many other interesting little bugs and birds – from ant-lions to natterjack toads. And the plants and flowers you'll find range from miniature orchids to imposing skunk cabbage. Come outside and enjoy our special places.

Many of our nature reserves and other wildlife areas have Visitor Centres where you can find out much more about what you're seeing (and hearing) in nature. Look us up on our website at www.nationaltrust.org.uk to find out what natural wonders are near to you.

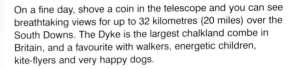

The Devil's Dyke
Countryside Walks

Devil's Dyke Road
Poynings
West Sussex
01273 857712

OPENING TIMES
All year

ADMISSION PRICES
Countryside free

On a fine day, shove a coin in the telescope and you can see breathtaking views for up to 32 kilometres (20 miles) over the South Downs. The Dyke is the largest chalkland combe in Britain, and a favourite with walkers, energetic children, kite-flyers and very happy dogs.

A devil of a story
Rumour has it that the dramatic valley cut into the chalk was dug by the Devil in an attempt to flood the churches. Trouble is, he only had until sunrise to do his dastardly deed. Halfway through, he spied a candle in a window and heard a cock crow – fooled into thinking dawn had arrived, he scarpered without finishing the job.

What to see
- Look up at dare-devil hang-gliders floating through the sky.
- Look down to spot exotic orchids and nice-smelling herbs in the grass.
- Look out for information panels explaining the great views.

What to do
- Pedal your bike along the bridlepaths.
- Follow one of the self-guided walking tours – pick up our 'Delve into the Dyke' leaflet.
- Take the hugely popular route 77 bus from Brighton Pier to the Dyke (or back).

Special events
We have activities like Ugly Bug or Orchid Safaris and Devil's Dyke Detectives, and you can also go on one of our working holidays, get in touch to see what's on.

By the way...
- There's a very family-friendly pub by the car park, with great grub.
- There's a classic open-top bus service on Sundays and Bank holidays–pick up our 'Breeze up to the Dyke' leaflet.
- There are car parks right there, and an information trailer during the season.

Ightham Mote
Historic house   Walks

Ightham Mote is a romantic moated medieval and Tudor manor house, built around a courtyard. It's so hidden away that even Cromwell's soldiers got lost trying to find it in the dark, and looted a nearby house instead. The Mote started life in 1320 but has been added to by various owners, including the Selby family, who lived in it from the end of the Elizabethan period right through to Victorian times. Over the years it has acquired a painted Tudor ceiling, a Jacobean fireplace, 18th-century wallpaper and a 19th-century billiards room.

Remember remember...
The story goes that Dame Dorothy Selby sent a letter warning Lord Monteagle not to attend Parliament on 5th November 1605 – the night of the Gunpowder Plot. But her letter gave the game away, and supporters of Guy Fawkes were so angry that they locked her in a secret room in the house, and left her there to die. Years later, some workmen discovered some bones. Who knows if they are Dame Dorothy's, but perhaps if you notice a chill in the air, you'd better watch out – just to be on the safe side.

What to see
- Perhaps the only house with a Grade I-listed dog kennel, made in 1890 for Dido, a St Bernard dog who was so big her food had to be served in a washing-up bowl.
- All those owners had different building ideas and no building restrictions, so look out for about 7 different types of chimneys.
- There's a slit in the wall near the entrance gate, known as a parley hole. In medieval days people would post letters or speak through it to ask if they could come into the building.

Mote Road, Ivy Hatch,
Sevenoaks, Kent, TN15 0NT
01732 810378

South & South East

OPENING TIMES
House
12 Mar–29 Oct
10.30am–5.30pm
Mon, Wed–Fri, Sun

Garden
12 Mar–29 Oct 10am–5:30pm
Mon, Wed–Fri, Sun

Estate
Open daily all year, dawn to dusk

Restaurant
9 Feb–11 Mar 11am–3pm
Thur–Sat.
12 Mar–29 Oct 10am–5.30pm
Mon, Wed–Fri, Sun.
2 Nov–23 Dec 11am–3pm
Thur–Sat

Last admission
30mins before closing time

Notes:
Booking at restaurant advised in winter and evenings, please tel. for opening times outside property hours

ADMISSION PRICES
£8.50, child £4, family £21.00.
Groups £7.50, child £3.50

continued...   51

What to do

- Squint through the squint window in the Chapel. And what on earth is a putlog?
- Try and hug the massive sweet chestnut trees, which measure over 8 metres (23 feet) around.
- Explore the gardens, which provided the medieval house with food. The Bowling Green used to be a large fish pond!
- Find out about medieval crafts and life from the exhibitions and displays.

Special events

There are many different events during the season, and quite a few are suitable for all the family. Recent activities have included woodcarving and cookery demonstrations and special drawing workshops for children. Some children's activities involve a small additional fee. It's a good idea to phone first to see what's on, and booking is sometimes necessary.

By the way...

- Ightham Mote was the subject of the largest conservation project ever undertaken by the National Trust on a house of this kind, which started in 1988 and was only finished in 2004.
- Contact us in advance for information on the wide range of touchable objects. There are many scented plants in the Herb walk.
- Wheelchairs are available, as well as a portable ramp. Some of the grounds and upper floors of the house are not accessible easily.

The Needles Old Battery
Fort

This Victorian fort is perched on the tip of the Isle of Wight in a stunning position overlooking The Needles rocks. If you have an interest in guns, ships and military matters, there's a lot of interest to explore here.

Battered about a bit
Did you know that a Battery is simply a collection of guns and artillery? In 1903 the obsolete guns were thrown over the cliff. Tsk! Later on, early anti-aircraft guns were tried out here and even rocket tests in the 1950s and '60s. Don't worry, nothing's loaded now.

What to see
- Cartoons by wartime artist Geoff Campion, which explain what went on at the Old Battery.
- A list of all the ships that have been wrecked on The Needles.
- Original cannons on display.

What to do
- Go through the 55-metre (60 yard) tunnel to view The Needles.
- Climb up the narrow spiral staircase to the searchlight when you get there.
- Learn how to use the Beaufort Scale to know how strong the wind is – it'll blow you away!

Special events
Though we don't have many events we have an exhibition, and you might want to visit the nearby Bembridge Windmill while you're here – you can climb right up to the top.

By the way...
- We're afraid this site is somewhat inaccessible if you have mobility problems. The paths are steep and can be uneven. But the ground floor is accessible.
- The walk up to the Old Battery is 1.6 kilometres (roughly 1 mile) – so be prepared for a bit of a hike.

West Highdown, Totland, Isle of Wight, PO39 0JH
01983 754772

OPENING TIMES
Battery, tearoom
26 Mar–29 Jun 10.30am–5pm
Mon–Thur, Sat, Sun
1 Jul–31 Aug 10.30am–5pm
Daily
2 Sep–29 Oct 10.30am–5pm
Mon–Thur, Sat, Sun

Tea-room only
13 Jan–18 Mar 07
11am–4.30pm, Sat, Sun

Notes
Open Good Fri. Property closes in bad weather; tel. on day of visit to check

ADMISSION PRICES
£3.90, child £1.95

Petworth House

Historic house   Park   Lake

Petworth, West Sussex,
GU28 0AE. 01798 342207

OPENING TIMES

House
1 Apr–29 Oct 11am–5pm Mon-
Wed, Sat, Sun

Shop, Restaurant
18 Mar–29 Mar 11pm–4pm
Mon–Wed, Sat, Sun
1 Apr–29 Oct 11am–5pm
Mon–Wed, Sat, Sun
1 Nov–16 Dec 10am–3.30pm
Wed–Sat
17 Dec–20 Dec 10am–3.30pm
Mon–Wed, Sun

Park
All year 8am–Dusk Daily

Pleasure Ground & kitchens
18 Mar–29 Mar 11pm–4pm
Mon–Wed, Sat, Sun
1 Apr–29 Oct 11am–6pm
Mon–Wed, Sat, Sun
1 Nov–16 Dec 10am–3.30pm
Wed–Sat

Notes
Open Good Fri. Please note:
Extra rooms shown weekdays
(but not BH Mons) as follows:
Mon, White & Gold Room and
White Library; Tues & Wed,
three bedrooms on first floor.
Park: closed afternoons of
open-air concerts

ADMISSION PRICES

£8.00, child £4.00, family £20.00.
Groups £7.00

Pleasure Ground only
£3.00, child £1.50

A magnificent 17th-century house and grounds with landscaping by
'Capability' Brown and more than 1000 fallow deer – probably the
largest herd in Britain. The house is full of treasures and has the
National Trust's finest collection of paintings – including 19 paintings
by Turner, who lived here for a while. It is still the home of Lord and
Lady Egremont, but visitors can explore quite a bit of the house and
grounds.

I do, I do, I do – but don't sit down!

Elizabeth Percy, who inherited Petworth in 1682, married three times
before she was 16. Her third husband, the Duke of Somerset, was so
full of his own importance that he cut one of their daughters out of his
will because she dared to sit down while he was asleep!

What to see

- A very fancy Victorian kitchen a huge display of copper cookware.
- Fascinating limewood carvings by Grinling Gibbons (great name!).
- Murals on the very imposing Grand Staircase, and paintings and
  sculptures all over.

What to do

- Visit the little cemetery for the family pets, on the lawn near the North
  Gallery. There's also a statue of the 3rd Earl of Egremont's favourite
  dog by the lake.
- Follow the underground passage the servants took from kitchen to
  dining room.
- Watch the deer – they are actually quite tame, but please don't
  disturb them. If a fawn is left on its own, please don't pick it up –
  Mum is probably coming back any minute and will be very worried if
  you're there.

Special events
Recently we've had murder mystery events (suitable for all), guided walks of the stables and storytelling events. There's a lot on – get in touch to see what's coming up.

By the way...
- There are wheelchairs available, and a ramped entrance. There are steps to the upper floors and elsewhere.
- Lots of touchable objects, just ask the Room Stewards as you go round.
- Baby-changing facilities and a children's menu.

Polesden Lacey

Historic house   Garden   Walks

Great Bookham, nr Dorking,
Surrey, RH5 6BD
01372 452048

OPENING TIMES

House
12 Apr–29 Oct 11am–5pm
Wed–Sun

Garden, Shop, Tea-room
1 Mar–29 Oct 11am–5pm Daily
30 Oct–23 Dec 11am–4pm
Daily
3 Jan–28 Feb 07 11am–4pm
Daily

Notes
Open BH Mons (11am–5pm).
Garden: closes dusk if earlier.
Shop & tearoom may be closed
for short periods during the
year due to refurbishment.
Shop closed for stock-taking
3 & 4 Jan 07

ADMISSION PRICES
£9.00, child £4.50, family
£22.50. Groups £7.65

Grounds only
£6.00, child £3.00, family £15.00
Croquet lawns and equipment
for hire from house (see right)

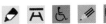

Step back into the 1920s, stroll through the house and grounds and imagine you're a house guest of the Hon Mrs Greville, a society hostess who lived here. In 1923 the future King George VI and Queen Elizabeth spent some of their honeymoon in this elegant Regency villa, and must have enjoyed its opulent interiors and beautiful rose garden.

Party party...
Mrs Greville threw many lavish parties for the rich and famous and entertained all kinds of royalty. She came from quite humble origins as the daughter of William McEwan – founder of the brewery. This was just her country home – she had another one for her London parties.

What to see
- Lady G's mementoes from her parties, kept in a special book – you can even find out what her guests had to eat.
- Gleaming gilt-covered walls and a chandelier with nearly 4000 pieces that takes over a week to clean.
- Lovely gardens – find Lady Greville's gravestone in the rose garden.

What to do
- Croquet anyone? Have a go on the croquet lawn, you can hire equipment from us (please book in advance).
- Test your brains with the house quiz.
- Run around in the children's play area and try the adventure trail.

Special events
There are often events in the grounds, including sheepdog trials and vintage car rallies. We have fungus forays and spooky Halloween events, as well as a summer festival with children's events. Get in touch.

By the way...
- There are wheelchairs available, and a ramped entrance. There are steps to the upper floors and elsewhere.
- Call first, and we'll arrange touchable objects for you to try.
- Baby-changing, children's menu and hip-carrying child slings available.

Sheffield Park Garden
Garden   Lakes   Walks

This lovely 'Capability' Brown garden is nowhere near Sheffield. Sheffield means 'sheep clearing', and the park is actually recorded first in the Domesday book. The 49 hectares (120 acres) of gardens has foxes, kingfishers and rabbits – and many secret areas as well as wide open spaces to run about in.

Lady of the lake
According to legend there's a lady ghost between the third and fourth lakes, known as Upper and Lower Woman's Way Pond. You could wave, but she wouldn't see you – apparently she has no head!

What to see
* In spring there are tons of daffodils and bluebells, and Autumn is pretty fantastic too.
* Swans, herons, hares, frogs, dormice....but probably not all at once.
* Waterfalls, cascades and four large lakes (and the odd duck – well, more than one odd duck).

What to do
* Parade down the Big Tree Walk and see the massive American trees which escaped a big storm in 1987.
* Get all clever, and learn to identify trees by doing the tree trail walk.
* The Bluebell Steam Railway is just up the road, and there's a joint ticket you can buy to combine it with your visit.

Special events
Have a go at weaving, spinning and making metal tools at a Victorian weekend, or take part in a teddy bear's picnic. Telephone us to check what's on.

By the way...
* Baby-changing facilities. Pushchairs and back-carriers are fine, and we can loan you an all-terrain pushchair or back carrier.
* No doggies, it's just not really suitable.
* Four wheelchairs available and a map of an accessible route. Some of the grounds have steep slopes.

Sheffield Park, East Sussex, TN22 3QX. 01825 790231

OPENING TIMES
Garden & Shop
14 Feb–26 Feb 10.30am–4pm Tue–Sun
28 Feb–30 Apr 10.30am–6pm Tue–Sun
1 May–4 Jun 10.30am–6pm Daily
6 Jun–1 Oct 10.30am–6pm Tue–Sun
2 Oct–31 Oct 10.30am–6pm Tue–Sun
1 Nov–23 Dec 10.30am–4pm Tue–Sun
27 Dec–31 Jan 10.30am–4pm Wed–Sun
6 Jan–11 Feb 10.30am–4pm Sat, Sun
13 Feb–25 Feb 07 10.30am–4pm Tue–Sun

Notes
Open BH Mons, last admission 1hr before closing

ADMISSION PRICES
£6.20, child £3.10, family £15.50. Joint ticket with Bluebell Railway available. Individual RHS members free

Witley & Milford Commons

Heaths   Woodland   Visitor Centre

Witley Centre,Witley,
Godalming, Surrey, GU8 5QA
01428 683207

OPENING TIMES

Centre
25 Mar–29 Oct 11am–5pm
Sat, Sun, 11am–4pm Tue–Fri

Common
Open all year, daily.

Notes
Open BH Mons and Good Fri
11am–5pm

ADMISSION PRICES
Free

Here you'll find one of the few remaining fragments of the heath that used to cover much of Southern England. Used as common land over many generations, since the Bronze Age, Witley Common has several ancient burial mounds, and evidence of iron working from the 16th and 17th century. Today the commons provide a sanctuary for wildlife and also for a chance for you to escape from the hustle-bustle, walk the trails, or watch birds at the bird-tables while you picnic outside the purpose-built Centre.

Left right, left right
During the First and Second World Wars, the commons were used as a training camp for the army. There were up to 20,000 soldiers marching around on it at one time. A Polish contingent of soldiers planted Hawthorn around their barracks, to cheer things up a bit. In the late 1940s, the parade ground was broken up, and the land was restored to its pre-war condition. Now the commons are a Site of Special Scientific Interest.

What to see
- The Green Hairstreak and Silver-Studded Blue. No, they're not punks, they're butterflies!
- Woodpeckers and nuthatches on Witley Common.
- Dartford warblers and Nightingales on Milford Common.
- Lizards, Adders and Roe Deer.

What to do
- Bring a picnic and relax.
- Pick up a quiz sheet from the Witley Centre and go on one of the nature trails over heathland and woodland.
- Visit the countryside exhibition and try out the special puzzles and quizzes for the younger members of the family.
- Have a cup of tea and watch the wildlife.

Special Events
Get in touch to find out what events we have on. Past activities have included Pond Dipping for bugs and creepy crawlies, and a Night Hike for Bats. Booking is essential, and children must bring an adult along too.

By the way...
- The grounds are partly accessible, but it can be a bit muddy in wet weather. There are two wheelchairs available at the Witley Centre, as well as an adapted WC. The Shop and picnic tables are accessible.
- There's a touch table of objects you can handle, and a guide in Braille.

Ham House

Ham House is unique in Europe as the most complete survival of 17th-century fashion and power. One of a series of palaces and grand houses along the banks of the Thames, it was built in 1610 and enlarged in the 1670s, when it was at the heart of Restoration court life and intrigue.

Spooky stories

Ham House was home to the extravagant Duchess of Lauderdale, who was renowned as a political schemer during the Civil War and Restoration period. She is said to still haunt its passageways. In fact, there are so many phantom tales of Ham, that it is reported to be one of the most haunted houses in England.

What to see

- The lavish 17th-century interiors with a wealth of textiles, furniture and paintings.
- Visit the service buildings. See the earliest identified Still House in England and the dairy with cast iron 'cows legs'.

Ham Street, Ham, Richmond-upon-Thames TW10 7RS
0208 9401950

London & East

OPENING TIMES
House
25 Mar–29 Oct 1pm–5pm
Mon–Wed, Sat & Sun

Garden
All year 11am–6pm Mon–Wed, Sat & Sun

Café
7 Jan–19 Mar 11am–4pm
Sat & Sun

Shop/café
25 Mar–29 Oct 11am–5:30pm
Mon–Wed, Sat & Sun
4 Nov–17 Dec 11am–4pm
Sat & Sun

Café
6 Jan 07–18 Mar 07
11am—4pm Sat & Sun

Notes
Open Good Fri: house 1am–5pm; garden 11am–6pm. Garden: closes at dusk if earlier; closed 25, 26 Dec & 1 Jan. Christmas lunches in Dec, illuminated evening openings in Dec for garden/shop/café.

ADMISSION PRICES
£8, child £4, family £19. Groups £7. Group visits outside normal hours £9. NT members: £5.50. Garden only: £4, child £2, family £9.

What to do

- There are ghost tours from end of October and family ghost tours throughout the school holidays. But booking is essential so phone in advance.
- Ham is a festive place in the Christmas season: there are Family Carol Concerts and a chance to see how servants would have celebrated 'below stairs'.
- Walk through the 250 trees that comprise the impressive tree avenues.

Special Events

Ham House hosts many talks and tours throughout the year, so look on the internet site for what's coming up.

Morden Hall Park & Snuff Mill

Waterways Meadows Environmental Centre

It's not often you can find a huge park so near a London Underground station. And Morden Hall's parkland is not your average back garden, with over 50 hectares (125 acres) of rose garden, meadows and wetlands to explore. A river runs through it – follow its meanders and bridges and you'll come to the two water mills, used until 1922 to grind snuff. You can still see the original waterwheel that turned the millstones to crush the tobacco. Morden Hall itself, built in 1770 and owned by Westminster Abbey, is now a popular restaurant.

Something a bit fishy

The park was home to Gilliat Hatfield, a keen huntsman and fisherman, who enjoyed the idea of being a country gentleman. But he preferred living in the cottage in the grounds to the Hall. He was happy to build a big stable block for his hunting horses as well as other buildings. And in keeping with his love of all things fishin', he converted the Dairy for trout breeding. The weather vane on top of the stables is also – you guessed it – a trout.

What to see

- Coots, moorhens and herons on the waterways.
- All kinds of fish in the Capital Garden Centre's aquaria.
- Outside the mill, two of the millstones that used to grind the tobacco.

What to do

- Wander by the River Wandle, and cross the variety of bridges crossing the river. Pick up a leaflet at the National Trust shop.
- Have a picnic in the fenced dog-free paddock especially for families.
- Visit the independently run Deen City Farm (at the northern edge of the park), where you can stroke rabbits and guinea pigs, and see baby goats, Jacob sheep and Derek, the snow-white peacock. Usually open Tuesday–Sunday.
- In season, smell the roses – there are over 2000 of them so that's quite a sniff – or should that be snuff…

Special Events

Snuff Mill Environmental Centre runs all sorts of activities, including a nature club, holiday activities and birthday parties with a natural theme. Call to find out what's on when you plan your visit.

By the way…

- The park is ideal for family cycling because it's flat, and the Wandle Trail passes right through it.
- Well-behaved dogs will enjoy a run in the parkland, but must be kept on leads near buildings and in the rose garden.
- The shop and café are accessible, but some of the paths in the park are not. There is recently improved access to the Snuff Mill, as well as an adapted WC.
- Braille and large print guides, and interesting things to hear and smell.
- There are baby-changing facilities, and the Riverside Café has a children's menu.

Morden Hall Road, Morden,
London, SM4 5JD
020 8545 6850

OPENING TIMES

Park
Open all year, 8am–6pm. Daily.

Shop and Café
Open all year, 10am–5pm. Daily.

Last admission
30mins before closing time.

Notes
Extra information on opening: Car park by café, shop and garden centre closes at 6pm. Shop and café closed 25, 26 Dec & 1 Jan. Rose Garden and estate buildings area open 8am–6pm. Please note that the farm and garden centre are not run by the NT.

ADMISSION PRICES

Free

61

Osterley Park

Historic house Lake Park

Jersey Road, Isleworth,
London, TW7 4RB
020 8232 5050

OPENING TIMES

House
5 Mar–26 Mar 1pm–4.30pm
Sat, Sun
23 Mar–29 Oct 1pm–4.30pm
Wed–Sun

Shop
4 Mar–26 Mar 1pm–5.30pm
Sat, Sun
29 Mar–30 Jul 1pm–5.30pm
Wed–Sun
31 July–3 Sep 1pm–5.30pm
Daily
6 Sep–29 Oct 1pm–5.30pm
Wed–Sun
1 Nov–17 Dec 12pm–4pm
Wed–Sun

Tea-room
Pls see website

Park, pleasure grounds
All year 9am–7.30pm Daily

Notes
Open BH Mons. On Sats house
may operate guided tours only.
Tel. property during week prior
to visiting for details

ADMISSION PRICES
House: £5.10, child £2.50,
family £12.80

Park & pleasure grounds
free

Osterley is a beautiful house and park within hitting distance of
central London, so a great place to escape the city to commune with
rabbits, squirrels and even parakeets. Originally Tudor, it was
transformed in the 18th century to its present elegant appearance.

Heartbreak house
In 1782 the 18-year-old daughter of the house ran away to Gretna
Green to marry the Earl of Westmorland. Soon afterwards her dad died,
some say of a broken heart.

What to see
- 400-year-old oaks, and neo-classical garden buildings in the park.
- A very flouncy bed in the state bedroom, designed by Robert Adam
  – not your average duvet!
- The 16th-century stables, still in use and sometimes open on
  Sunday afternoons.

What to do
- If the servants' quarters are open – check first – explore life 'below
  stairs'.
- The marigold was the emblem of the Child family, who lived here.
  Look for it in the garden, but also in decorations around the house.
- Look at the dirty 'before' patch on the wall in the Etruscan Room. It
  shows what it was like before the NT did their work on the house.

Special events

There are family fun days in the summer, and many other events. Past events include Christmas tree decoration, and tours of parts of the house that are usually closed, including the roof! You need to book.

By the way...

There's a waymarked trail around the park, and dogs on leads are welcome there.

We have baby-changing facilities, and pushchairs are admitted.

There's a 'hands on' exhibition and staff are always happy to describe objects to those who can't see them well.

Sutton House

Historic house

2 & 4 Homerton High Street,
Hackney, London, E9 6JQ
020 8986 2264

OPENING TIMES

Historic rooms & Art gallery
2 Feb–22 Dec 12.30pm (Gallery
12)–4.30pm Thur–Sat

Shop, Café-bar
As Art Gallery

Notes
Open BH Mons

ADMISSION PRICES
£2.50, child 50p, family £5.50

Here's an unexpected gem of a Tudor house, hidden right in the middle of East London. It's well worth a visit to explore its atmospheric interior, enjoy the peaceful courtyard and grab a bite to eat at the cosy café.

Hackney house

Difficult to believe that Hackney was once a pretty village outside London, but it was in 1535 when the house was built! Sutton House has been a rich merchant's home, a school, and a recreation for poor working men. Now it's a venue for concerts and art exhibitions.

What to see

- Fine Tudor oak panelling and carved fireplaces.
- Doors and panels that open to reveal parts of the original house – including two 'garderobe' loos – no longer in use!
- Paintings and artwork by local artists.

What to do

- Creep around in the old cellars.
- Explore the exhibition that tells the story of the house.
- Touch (and smell!) objects in the authentic Tudor kitchen.

Special events

We have many events, often family-friendly. Come on a ghost tour (if you dare!) or enjoy children's activities at our Craft Fair.

By the way...

- There's a children's quiz/trail and baby-changing facilities. Pushchairs are fine.
- We have a wheelchair – you need to book it – but there are stairs to upper floors.
- Worth checking that we're open to the public before you visit – there are sometimes special private events.

Belton House

This magnificent country house was build in 1685–89 for 'Young' Sir John Brownlow, and it's thought that the architect of St Paul's Cathedral, Sir Christopher Wren, had a hand in its H-shaped design. There are fine paintings and carvings inside, and 36 acres of gardens, with a beautiful Lakeside Walk.

Belting around Belton

Belton was the film location for the BBC's *Pride and Prejudice* as well as the children's serial Moondial. And you can act up too – there's Victorian clothing for all the family to try on. Take it off to play in our other attraction – the National Trust's largest adventure playground.

What to see

- Look out for all the animals used in the decorations and paintings in the house.
- Look up to see some very ornate ceilings.
- Look down to find a fancy painted floor in one of the rooms.

Grantham, Lincolnshire, NG32 2LS. 01476 566116

OPENING TIMES

House
25 Mar–29 Oct 12.30pm–5pm
Wed–Sun

Garden/playground
25 Mar–30 Jul 11am–5.30pm
Wed–Sun
1 Aug–31 Aug 10.30–5pm Daily
1 Sept–29 Oct 11–5.30pm
Wed–Sun

Garden
3 Nov–17 Dec 12pm–4pm
Fri–Sun
4 Feb–26 Feb 07 12pm–4pm
Sat & Sun

Shop, Restaurant
25 Mar–29 Oct 11am–5.15pm
Wed–Sun
3 Nov–17 Dec 12pm–4pm
Fri–Sun
4 Jan–26 Feb 12pm–4pm Sat, Sun

Notes
Open BH Mons. Property closed 15 July. Bellmount Woods: daily, access from separate car park

ADMISSION PRICES
£8, child £4.50, family £22.50. Groups £6.50

What to do
- Visit the activity room upstairs to try on costumes.
- Or the stableyard, with a Wildlife Discovery area.
- Swing, climb and slide away around the mega-sized adventure playground – the less energetic can watch from the picnic area!

Special events
Get in touch to see when our next family days are. We often have special walks, or even a chance to try your hand at crafts or archery.

By the way...
- Grab a family guide or activity pack to help you explore.
- Very baby-friendly, with facilities and carriers to borrow.
- Wheelchairs available but there are many steps up to the entrance. Map of accessible route in grounds.

Blickling Hall, Garden & Park

Historic house   Garden   Lake   Park

Blickling Hall is a quirky-looking building and has a sumptuous collection of Dutch gables and turrets, striking brick chimneys and some massive yew hedges. The present building was built in the early 17th century and is one of England's great Jacobean houses, with a spectacular long gallery, and fine collections of pictures, books and tapestries. Wander in its extensive gardens and parklands, with something to see throughout the year and lots of interesting walks to explore.

Heads or tales

Henry VIII's second queen, poor old Anne Boleyn, lived in an earlier house at Blickling when she was young. Bet she later wished she'd stayed at home instead of marrying Henry, who had her beheaded. Some swear they've seen her headless ghost riding up to the house, in a coach pulled by headless horses.

What to see

- Anne Boleyn's life-size statue on the stairs (with head!).
- Some very curious beasts hiding in the plaster ceiling in the long gallery.
- A secret garden with a sun dial.
- A pyramid. Well, not a real Egyptian one but a tomb – or mausoleum – built for one of Blickling's owners.

What to do

- Explore the park by following one of 3 waymarked walks. Rover can come too if kept on a lead.
- Have a picnic in the orchard, or by the visitor reception area.
- See if you can spot local wildlife, including woodpeckers, bitterns and owls.

Blickling, Norwich, Norfolk, NR11 6NF. 01263 738030

OPENING TIMES

House
25 Mar–29 Jul 1pm–5pm Wed–Sun
30 Jul–3 Sept 1pm–5pm Mon, Wed–Sun
6 Sept–1 Oct 1pm–5pm Wed–Sun
4 Oct–29 Oct 1pm–4pm Wed–Sun

Garden
25 Mar–29 Jul 10.15am–5.15pm Wed–Sun
30 Jul–3 Sep 10.15am–5.15pm Mon, Wed–Sun
6 Sep–29 Oct 10.15am–5.15pm Wed–Sun
2 Nov–24 Mar 11am–4pm Thur–Sun

Park
Open all year Dawn–dusk Daily

Shop, Restaurant & Bookshop
As for garden

Art galleries
19 Mar–30 Oct 11am–4.30pm Wed–Sun

Notes
Open BH Mons. Cycle hire also available Wed–Sun during school hols March–Oct, 10.15am–5.15pm

ADMISSION PRICES
£8, child £4, family (one adult) £12. Groups £6.80

Garden only
£5, child £2.50. Groups £4.20
Coarse fishing in lake; permits available at lakeside

continued…   67

Special Events
We have quite a lot of family-friendly events. Recent activities have included Sculpture workshops, August Antics, with giant garden games and arts and crafts for children of all ages, and Blickling Bird Bonanza, a chance to make a bird feeder and create a mythical bird. There's lots going on, for children and would-be children. Get in touch to book.

By the way...
- At the weekends you can hire bicycles to explore the park.
- The basement rooms are not accessible except by stairs, but the rest of the house is, and we have wheelchairs available. The Grounds and other facilities are fully accessible, with maps of special routes.
- We have Braille and large print guides, and a handling collection.

Dunstable Downs

The Downs are a large area of chalk grassland and farmland that's a haven for wildlife. A great place to stretch your legs and get lots of fresh air. It's the highest spot in Bedfordshire and has wonderful views out over the Vale of Aylesbury and along the Chiltern Ridge. The Icknield Way is possibly the oldest road in England.

Downs in disguise
During World War II the Meteorological Office at Dunstable was camouflaged to look like part of the Downs. The buildings and tennis court were covered with leaves and nets, and one of the buildings was disguised as a haystack!

What to see
- Flying of all kinds – planes on their way to Luton, gliders, paragliders and kites.
- Or put your nose to the ground to look for interesting plants and creatures.

What to do
- A very popular kite-flying spot. If you don't have one, we sell a large range in the shop.
- Pop into the popular Countryside Visitor Centre, a very family friendly place.
- Bring your bike – the bridleway is ok for cycling.

By the way...
- The Centre is fully accessible and a popular family place.
- Baby-changing facilities.

Whipsnade Road, Kensworth, Dunstable, Bedfordshire, LU6 2TA. 01582 608489

OPENING TIMES

Downs
Open all year Daily

Shop
25 Mar–29 Oct 10.30am–5pm Mon–Fri
25 Mar–29 Oct 10–5pm Sat
25 Mar–29Oct 10–6pm Sun
30 Oct–18 Mar 07–10–4pm Sat, Sun

Kiosk
Open all year 10–dusk Daily

Note
Open BH and Good Fri. Countryside Centre opens weather permitting inc Sun and BHols. Kiosk closed 25 Dec

ADMISSION PRICES
Countryside free

Dunwich Heath & Beach

Coastal centre   Beach   Heath   Visitor centre

London & East

Dunwich, Saxmundham,
Suffolk, IP17 3DJ
01728 648505

OPENING TIMES

Reserve
Open all year during daylight hours. Daily

Shop and tea-room
Open from 10, closing times vary. Sometimes closed Mon, Tuesday. Open daily May half-term

ADMISSION PRICES
Car park charge for non-members

Dunwich is a remote and beautiful place with a unique atmosphere. There are stunning views out over the sea and mysterious heathland walks, shady woods and sandy cliffs to explore. It's a lovely place to walk, and then come back for tea at the old coastguard cottages.

A village in the sea
The original Dunwich town was a thriving medieval port. One night in 1328 a hurricane force wind shifted a spit of sand and made the harbour useless. Gradually the town became derelict, and over several hundred years it fell over the cliffs into the sea.

What to see
- The plans showing where Dunwich used to be.
- The last remains of a monastery, used for grazing sheep now.
- Rare wildlife, like the Dartford warbler and the ant-lion – a rather strange bug that hides in a hole.

What to do
- Splash in the sea, and pick up interesting pebbles on the beach.
- Go on one of the popular nature trails. Have a picnic. Fly a kite.
- Look out from the viewing room in the Coastguard Cottages.

By the way...
- We have holiday flats if you'd like to stay here longer.
- There are events in the school holidays for children ages 6–12.
- There are 'Have a Go' family days in August – try beach art.

Hatfield Forest

Ancient forest　Cycling　Fishing　Lakes　Walks

This ancient woodland is a rare surviving example of a medieval royal hunting forest. Today it's the haunt of picnickers and icecream eaters, as well as a great variety of wildlife. Fishing is available on the lake, and there's loads of room for dog-walking and playing a bit of football or Frisbee. All in all a great place for the whole family to relax royally.

Bunny trouble
In the 1930s there were more rabbits than visitors to the forest – over 1100 were once caught in a single week. Luckily the plans to exterminate all the deer never happened, and there are still around 100 of them out there in the woods – see if you can spot them peeking at you while you peek at them.

What to see
- During summer, cattle grazing in the forest.
- Ducks and the occasional swan on the lake.
- The newly restored Shell House – open at weekends.

What to do
- Get a day ticket to go fishing.
- Get on your bike – there are cycle routes throughout the forest.
- Walk about, sit around and have a cuppa.

Special events
Trusty, the National Trust Hedgehog, sometimes comes along to give out stickers, and we have Halloween and Christmas trails. We have quite a few live music and craft events. Get in touch to see what's on.

By the way...
- Hatfield is both a National Nature Reserve and a SSSI.
- The shop and visitor centre are fully accessible.
- Great place for picnics – but watch out for cowpats!

Takeley, nr Bishop's Stortford, Essex, CM22 6NE
01279 874040

OPENING TIMES
All year Dawn–Dusk Daily

Refreshments
25 Mar–31 Oct 10am–4.30pm Daily
5 Nov–25 Mar 07 10am–3.30pm Sat, Sun

Notes
Refreshments available daily in school holidays 1 Nov–31 Mar 10am–3.30pm

ADMISSION PRICES
Car park charge for non-members. Riding for members of Hatfield Forest Riding Association only, tel. for details

Houghton Mill

Ancient mill   Walks

Houghton, nr Huntingdon,
Cambridgeshire, PE28 2AZ
01480 301494

OPENING TIMES
25 Mar–30 Apr 11am–5pm
Sat, Sun
1 May–27 Sep 11am–5pm
Mon–Wed, Sat, Sun
1 Oct–29 Oct 11am–5pm
Sat, Sun

Bookshop, Tea-room
As for Mill

Walks/Car park
All year 9am–6pm Daily

Notes
Open BH Mons: Mill 1pm–5pm;
tea-room 11am–5pm and Good
Fri: 1pm–5pm. Caravan and
campsite open Mar–Oct.
Groups and school parties at
other times by arrangement

ADMISSION PRICES
£3.20, child £1.50, family £7.00.
Groups £2.00, child £1.00

Enjoy watching the wheels and cogs go round in this last working watermill on the Great Ouse, set on an island in the middle of the river. The impressive five-storey, 18th-century building has operational machinery, and you can see flour being produced before your eyes (and buy some to take home too). It's a lovely area to take a walk in, with riverside meadows and a trail around Houghton Village.

Watery power
Did you know that along with making flour, and pumping water, mills have also been used to produce paper and even gunpowder? The only milling that goes on at Houghton is of the floury variety although the water also drives a turbine that produces electricity for the building.

What to see
- All the water wheels, grinding stones, cogs and shafts – great if you're interested in how things work.
- Milling (on Sundays and Bank Holidays).Find out what a damsel or hopper was for.
- Look out on the nearby lock.

What to do
- Have a go at turning the model millstones and pulling on the rope to lift a bag of flour.
- Bike or horse-ride on the bridle-way (but watch out if you're walking!).
- Stay in the nearby caravan and campsite (run by the Caravan Club).

By the way...
- The grounds are fully accessible, as is the ground floor of the mill.
- Phone ahead to make sure we're going to be milling if you want to see the wheel in action.

Ickworth House & Park

This very eccentric stately home, with a big central rotunda and curved corridors, was built in 1795 by an equally eccentric bloke, the 4th Earl of Bristol. Today you can see his fine Georgian silver, and paintings by Titian, Gainsborough and Velásquez. The fine 18th-century parkland is also worth exploring, with an Italianate garden, a vineyard, canal and lake.

Hervey going

Frederick August Hervey, aka the 4th Earl of Bristol was Bishop of Derry for 35 years, but also enjoyed generally living it up. Lord Chesterfield said 'At the beginning God created three different species, men, women, and Herveys,' and Lord Charlemont added 'His genius is like a shallow stream, rapid, noisy, diverting, but useless'. With friends like that...

What to see

- An unusual collection of tree stumps and massive stones from the Giant's Causeway
- Silver fish, fans, miniature paintings and lots of other objects.
- Look out on the nearby lock.

What to do

- Play on the adventure playground.
- Follow a family trails or a cycle route through the grounds.
- Spot some deer from the deer hide.

Ickworth, The Rotunda, Horringer, Bury St Edmunds, Suffolk, IP29 5QE
01284 735270

London & East

OPENING TIMES

House
20 Mar–1 Oct 1pm–5pm Mon, Tues, Fri–Sun
2 Oct–5 Nov 1pm–4.30pm Mon, Tues, Fri–Sun

Garden
20 Mar–1 Oct 10am–5pm Mon, Tues, Fri–Sun
2 Oct–18 Mar 07 10am–4pm Mon, Tues, Fri–Sun

Park
Open all year dawn–dusk Daily

Shop
20 Mar–5 Nov 12pm–5pm Mon, Tues, Fri–Sun
6 Nov–23 Dec 11am–4pm Mon, Tues, Fri–Sun
27 Dec–1 Jan 07 11am–4pm, Daily exc Tues

Restaurant
As for shop

Last admission
As shop

ADMISSION PRICES
£7, child £3. Groups £6, child £2.50

Park & garden only
(inc. access to shop & restaurant): £3.40, child 90p

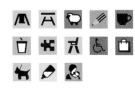

continued...   73

Special events

We often have guided family walks, sometimes led by previous ghostly inhabitants, and you can learn about Echo the Bat and his batty friends. Get in touch to see if we have an event coming up.

By the way...

- We're doing some building and conservation at the moment – the house is open as usual, but some of the grounds may not be at times.
- We have a ramp and three wheelchairs to help you get around the house. The shop and café do have quite a few steps.

Oxburgh Hall

Historic house   Garden   Woods

You might see a swan float past your window in this grand manor house surrounded by a moat, and complete with battlements. The Bedingfield family have lived here ever since the house was built in 1482.

Hidey-hole
After the Reformation, catholic families like the Bedingfields had a lot to fear, even death. The house has secret doors and a priest's hole, where they or their priest could hide if soldiers came.

What to see
- Look for the ha-ha – a ditch dug on the edge of a field to keep cows and sheep out. You can hardly see it, so don't fall in – ha ha!
- A huge Tudor gatehouse.
- The priests' hole – imagine how scary that would be.

What to do
- Take a peek at the little Catholic chapel in the grounds.
- Take the Woodland Explorer trail around the garden, or enjoy a lunch picnic in the park.
- Check out where the drawbridge used to be.

Special events
We have family events like Easter egg hunts, and also Living History days when you can meet a variety of characters in Tudor costume. Check with us to see what's on.

By the way…
- There's a secondhand bookshop in the NT shop, during season.
- Try out the children's quiz/trail and pick up information on self-guided family tours.
- Baby-changing facilities and children's menu.
- We have a ramped entrance and wheelchairs; there are stairs to other floors. And be careful near the moat!

Oxborough, King's Lynn,
Norfolk, PE33 9PS
01366 328258

OPENING TIMES
House
19 Mar–30 Oct 1pm–5pm
Mon–Wed, Sat, Sun

Garden, Shop, Garden
8 Jan–13 Mar 11am–4pm
Sat, Sun
19 Mar–31 Jul 11am–5.30pm
Mon–Wed, Sat, Sun
1 Aug–31 Aug 11am–5.30pm
Daily
3 Sep–30 Oct 11am–5.30pm
Mon–Wed, Sat, Sun
5 Nov–18 Dec, 7 Jan–26 Feb
11am–4pm Sat, Sun

Notes
Open BH Mons (11am–5pm
(inc. house). On Thur & Fri in
Aug, only shop, restaurant and
garden are open

ADMISSION PRICES
£6.50, child £3.25.

Garden & estate only
£3.00, child £1.50
Reduced rate when arriving by
cycle

Sutton Hoo

Archaeological site

Tranmer House, Sutton Hoo,
Woodbridge, Suffolk, IP12 3DJ
01394 389700

OPENING TIMES

**Exhibition Hall, Shop,
Restaurant**
25 Mar–29 Oct 11am–5pm
Daily, sometimes closed Mon &
Tues
4 Nov–17 Dec 11am–4pm Sat
& Sun
27 Dec–31 Dec 11–4pm
Wed–Sun
6 Jan–25 Mar 07 11am–4pm
Sat, Sun

Note
Open BH Mons. Open daily
during local half-terms. Estate
walks open daily all year round
11am–5pm (except for certain
Thurs Nov–Feb. Tel. Estate
office for details).

ADMISSION PRICES
£5.50, child £2.50, family
£13.50.
Reduced rate when arriving by
public transport, cycle or foot

Sutton Hoo is one of Britain's most important and atmospheric
archeological sites. It was the burial ground of the Anglo-Saxon
kings of East Anglia. Visit the award-winning exhibition that explains
the burial mounds and shows many of the finds from this
extraordinary place.

Underground treasure ship
In 1939 one of the large mounds at the site was excavated, revealing a
huge amount of priceless royal treasure inside the remains of a burial
chamber in a 27-metre (90-foot) ship. It's one of the most important
finds ever found in Britain, and is famous worldwide.

What to see
- Visit the viewing platform to see the large burial mounds, including
  the 'Treasure Mound'.
- A full-size reconstruction of the ship's burial chamber with copies of
  its treasures as they may have been – an ongoing project involving
  craftsmen from across the UK and beyond.
- Changing displays of some of the actual artifacts discovered in
  1939.

What to do
- Watch our specially commissioned film conjuring up the world of
  Anglo-Saxon kings, craftsmen and poets.
- Walk along the River Debden on waymarked trails – take binoculars
  if you can; there are lots of birds.
- Have fun in the children's play area, and try out the dressing-up box
  in the exhibition.

Special events
Our family events have included felt-making demonstrations,
Halloween Happenings (very spooky!) and crafts. Contact us to find
what's planned.

By the way...
- The shop sells a children's range based on Sutton Hoo artifacts.
- There are some tethering rings and water too, for doggy friends.
- We have wheelchairs, and a map of an accessible route, the
  entrance is level.

Tattershall Castle

Castle   Grounds

You can explore from the dungeons to the battlements in this very dramatic medieval tower, with walls as thick as a room. It was built in the 1400s for Ralph, Lord Cromwell, a wealthy adviser to King Henry VI, and over one million locally made bricks were required to build the tower and buildings. There was an earlier fortified castle but this one was really made mostly for show.

It's a moat point
Well two, actually – the original castle on this site had an outer and inner moat, which have been restored. One 'for best' – for entertaining guests and visitors, so they say – and one to keep out nasty enemy gatecrashers.

What to see
- One vast tower – with four great chambers with enormous Gothic fireplaces and lots of tapestries.
- The very eerie dungeons – go on, we dare you.

Tattershall, Lincoln, Lincolnshire, LN4 4LR. 01526 342543

OPENING TIMES
Castle
4 Mar–19 Mar 12pm–4pm
Sat, Sun
25 Mar–27 Sep 11am–5.30pm
Mon–Wed, Sat, Sun
30 Sept–2 Nov 11am–4pm
Mon–Wed, Sat, Sun
4 Nov–10 Dec 12pm–4pm Sat, Sun.

Shop
As for castle

Note
Open Good Fri. 11am–5.30pm. Last audio guide issued 90mins before closing each day

ADMISSION PRICES
£4, child £2, family £10. Groups £3.50, child £1.75

What to do

- Dress up and play with Tudor toys and medieval costumes.
- Grab our free audio guide to find out more about 15th-century life.
- Walk over the moats (by way of the bridges, that is).

Special events

Fancy a spot of brass rubbing? On some Sundays we'll let you loose on our collection for a small charge. We also have children's activity days and living history weekends, get in touch.

By the way...

- We have some touchable objects and a Braille guide too.
- There are stairs to the upper floors in the castle.

Wicken Fen

Nature reserve   Cottage   Visitor centre   Walks

Britain's oldest nature reserve, and a very special and ancient place. Once the whole of East Anglia was covered with fenland, which is a special kind of peaty wetland. Now this is the last 0.1% of natural fenland left. It's a haven for birds, plants, insects and all kinds of wildlife. Explore its lush green paths and visit the hides, or walk along the boardwalk (fine for pushchairs).

Not quite high and dry
Most of the fenland that was part of the Great Fen of East Anglia has now been drained and ploughed. That drainage made the level of the dry land fall, so that Wicken Fen is now left standing like an island, up to 2 metres (6½ feet) higher than the land around it.

What to see
Butterflies, birds, bugs, reptiles, and rare plants like fen violet and milk parsley.
Fen Cottage – a typical workers' dwelling built from products of the fen.

What to do
Put on your wellies (it can be wet!) and take one of the trails–pick up a guide at the visitor's centre.
Bring your binoculars – or hire some from us – to look at the birds from Tower Hide.
Have a very un-medieval ice cream after your walk!

Special events
We have quite a lot going on. Recently we have had bat and moth detection nights, ghosts walks, wildlife identification and a chance to try your hand at rush weaving.

By the way...
We have a couple of wheelchairs, and the boardwalk is accessible, as is the café and picnic area.

Lode Lane, Wicken, Ely, Cambridgeshire, CB7 5XP
01353 720274

OPENING TIMES

Reserve
All year Dawn–dusk Daily

Fen Cottage
2 Apr–22 Oct 2pm–5pm Sunday

Centre/shop
1 Mar–2 Apr 10am–5pm Tues–Sun
3 Apr–23 Apr 10am–5pm Daily
25 Apr–23 Jul 10am–5pm Tues–Sun
24 Jul–3 Sep 10am–5pm Daily
5 Sep–22 Oct 10am–5pm Tues–Sun
23 Oct–29 Oct 10am–5pm Daily
31 Oct–28 Feb 07 10am–4.30pm Tues–Sun

Café
1 Mar–29 Oct As Centre
4 Nov–25 Feb 07 10.30am–4pm Sat & Sun

Notes
Open BH Mons. Reserve: closed 25 Dec. Some paths are closed in very wet weather. Visitor centre and café may occasionally be closed in winter. Fen Cottage (showing the way of life c.1900) open BH Mons and some other days in summer

ADMISSION PRICES
£4.50, child £2. Groups £3.50

Wimpole Home Farm

Farm   Adventure playground   Park

Wimpole Hall, Arrington,
Royston, Cambridgeshire,
SG8 0BW. 01223 206000

OPENING TIMES

Farm, Café

4 Mar–12 Mar 11am–4pm
Sat, Sun
18 Mar–19 Jul 10.30am–5pm
Mon–Wed, Sat, Sun
22 Jul–31 Aug 10.30am–5pm
Mon–Thur, Sat, Sun
3 Sep–1 Nov 10.30am–5pm
Mon–Wed, Sat, Sun
4 Nov–17 Dec 11am–4pm
Sat, Sun
27 Dec–4 Jan 07 11am–4pm
Mon–Thur, Sat & Sun
6 Jan–25 Feb 11am–4pm
Sat, Sun

Notes

Open BH Mons and Good Fri
10.30am–5pm. Open Sat–Thur
during school Easter and half-
term holidays

ADMISSION PRICES

NT members

£3, child £2, family £9

Non-members

£6, child £4, family £18.

Joint ticket with Hall

£11, child £6, family £28 (inc NT
members)
Reduced rate when arriving by
public transport or cycle

Lots to see at this charming farm built by Sir John Soane in 1794 for the 3rd Earl of Hardwicke, who was potty about animals and agriculture. Wimpole is a working farm that's home to all types of rare breeds, which you can look at, touch and even feed. Nearby Wimpole Hall is also worth a visit, with a huge park to explore.

Come in number five!

If you come to Wimpole in April you'll see new-born lambs, and might even see one being born. Once the lambs are born, we give them trendy ear tags (they don't mind them!) and mum and her lambs all have the same number sprayed on their sides, so we know who belongs to who.

What to see

- Different breeds of sheep with strange names like Logthan, Soays, Portland's and Manx.
- Cows, pigs, goats, rabbits, chickens … a farm full of four-legged friends (and two-legged ones with beaks).
- Thatched buildings and a Victorian Dairy.

What to do

- Go on a wagon ride between Home Farm and Wimpole Hall, pulled by our lovely big Shire Horses – they're such gentle giants.
- Feed the goats or other animals – but don't bring food, buy special food from the shop (better for their tums).
- Cuddle a bunny in the corner for younger children with smaller animals, rabbits and guinea pigs…ahhh!

Special events

Wimpole Home Farm has many events, like lambing weekends, children's days and Meet Father Christmas. You can even have your birthday party here – just don't share your cake with the chickens! Visit our web site or give us a call.

By the way...

- Pushchairs and back-carriers welcome, and there is a children's play area.
- Book one of our 3 wheelchairs and bear in mind that there are some gravel areas.

Woolsthorpe Manor

Historic house   Discovery centre

23 Newton Way, Woolsthorpe-by-Colsterworth, nr Grantham, Lincolnshire, NG33 5NR
01476 860338

OPENING TIMES

House
4 Mar–26 Mar 1pm–5pm
Sat, Sun
29 Mar–1 Oct 1pm–5pm
Wed–Sun
7 Oct–29 Oct 1pm–5pm
Sat, Sun

Note
Open BHols and Good Fri:
1pm–5pm

ADMISSION PRICES
£4.50, child £2.20, family
£11.20, family (one adult) £6.70

The birthplace and family home of Sir Isaac Newton, the chap who discovered gravity when an apple fell on his head in this very garden. The apple tree's no more, though one of its descendants lives on. It's amazing to think that Newton had some of his most important and famous ideas in this modest little house.

Irritating Isaac
Newton may have been a clever-clogs but he was also known to be a bit cross and cantankerous. He was prone to disagree with royal astronomers, and had an argument with famous mathematician Leibniz that lasted over 15 years. Well, nobody said a genius has to be nice.

What to see
- A big display telling the story of the discovery of gravity. That's heavy!
- An edition of Newton's famous work *Principia,* first published in 1687. That's quite heavy too.
- All kinds of Newtonian gadgets in the shop.

What to do
- Wander around the orchards and paddocks.
- Visit the farm buildings with rare breed Lincoln Longwool sheep.
- Dip into the Science Discovery Centre, with a chance to look through telescopes, play with pendulums and more.

Special events
We have an apple day (well, we would….) and have had family learning days that take you back to the 17th century. Get in touch to see what's coming up.

By the way...
- There's a family guide and quiz/trail for you to have a go at. And pick up a leaflet to do a village walk.
- Baby-changing facilities, but bear in mind the café is small and has a limited selection (it's only open at weekends, too).
- You can book a wheelchair, though there are stairs to the upper floors.

Attingham Park

An elegant 18th-century mansion with a grand façade and swanky Regency interiors – originally the home of the 1st Lord Berwick. See how the other half lived as you admire the silver, furniture and paintings here. The park is also pretty grand, with nice river walks, a play area – and there's also Home Farm, on the edge of the estate.

Bigging it up....
There were lots of tricks to make the house seem bigger! The drive is winding, and goes by especially positioned trees, so that the grounds seem larger. The Main Drawing Room has mirrors at either end, to make the room go on forever. And there are false doors to give the illusion of extra rooms.

What to see
- The Boudoir Room – for the ladies to retreat to. Round and with 5 doors (2 fakes!), it is decorated with romantic cupids.
- The Picture Gallery by John Nash. Look at the picture of Queen Charlotte, whose face ages as you walk past it from left to right.
- The Octagon Room–once Lord Berwick's private 'quiet room'.

What to do
- Imagine being a servant who had to answer when one of the bells in the Bell Room went off – there was one for every room in the house!
- Hunt out the biggest salmon ever caught in Britain in the Tenant's Parlour.
- Dress up, learn to lay a fire or play games of the times in the Family Activity Room.

Special events
Food fayres, deer park rides and carriage parades are just some of our recent events, as well as special activities during holiday times. Get in touch!

By the way...
- There's a children's play area, baby-changing and feeding facilities and you can borrow a child sling. Children's menu in the tea-room.
- Visit the Environmental discovery room in the park to find out about the deer and birds.
- Ask for the alternative entrance if you have mobility problems, and we have wheelchairs available. Handling collection is available, and there are things to touch in the house.

Shrewsbury, Shropshire, SY4 4TP. 01743 708162

Central

OPENING TIMES
House
4 Mar–19 Mar 1pm–5pm
Sat–Sun
25 Mar–29 Oct 1pm–5pm
Mon–Tues, Fri–Sun   .

Deer park
1 Mar–29 Oct 10am–8pm Daily
4 Nov–25 Feb 07 10am–5pm
Sat, Sun

Shop, Tearoom
4 Mar–19 Mar 11.30am–5pm
Sat–Sun
25 Mar–29 Oct 11.30am–5pm
Mon–Tues, Fri–Sun
4 Nov–4 Mar 07 11.30am–4pm
Sat–Sun

Notes
Open BH Mons 11am–5pm
Closed 25 Dec. On house open days (Fri–Tues), 12pm–1pm Taster tours only

Last admission
1hr before closing.

ADMISSION PRICES
£6.50, child £3.25, family £16.25. groups £5.50, child £2.75.

Park & grounds only
£3.30, child £1.65, family £8.20

Baddesley Clinton

Historic house   Garden   Lake

Rising Lane, Baddesley
Clinton Village, Knowle,
Solihull, Warwickshire,
B93 0DQ. 01564 783294

OPENING TIMES

House
1 Mar–30 Apr 1.30pm–5pm
Wed–Sun
3 May–30 Sep 1.30pm–5.30pm
Wed–Sun
1 Oct–5 Nov 1.30pm–5pm
Wed–Sun

Grounds, Shop & Restaurant
1 Mar–30 Apr 12pm–5pm
Wed–Sun
3 May–30 Sep 12pm–5.30pm
Wed–Sun
1 Oct–5 Nov 12pm–5pm
Wed–Sun
8 Nov–10 Dec 12pm–4.30pm
Wed–Sun

Note
Admission by timed ticket to
house; visitors may then stay
until house closes if they wish.
Open BH Mons

ADMISSION PRICES
£6.80, child £3.40, family
£17.00, groups £5.80

Grounds only
(inc. access to restaurant &
shop): £3.40, child £1.70

Combined ticket for gardens
only (Baddesley Clinton &
Packwood House)
£4.90, child £2.45
Combined ticket to both
Baddesley Clinton and
Packwood House £9.80, child
£4.90, family £24.50, groups
£8.40

In Elizabethan times this house was riddled with secret hidey-holes
to conceal the hounded Catholic Ferrers family and their friends. See
if you can spot them, then stretch your legs in the many walks and
trails in the grounds.

Not the most pleasant paddle
When Protestant Elizabeth I was on the throne, the house became a
refuge for Catholic priests on the run. In 1591 a priests' hole in the
drains saved nine catholic priests, who stood knee-deep in water while
the Queen's soldiers searched the house.

What to see
- The Ferrers family coat of arms in the 16th-century stained glass.
- Look carefully by the library fireplace to find a bloodstain from a
  murder that took place in 1483. Listen carefully too, for ghostly
  whispering!
- A 16th-century garderobe or loo, that hides the entrance to one of
  the secret hiding places.

What to do
- Find two other priest's holes – ask a steward to help you find
  them!
- Have a look at the moat – but watch out, don't fall in!
- Listen out for the chiming turret clock, and cosy up to our log fire in
  March and October.

EDWARD FERRERS LORD OF
BADDESLEY CLINTON MARRIED
THE LADY HARRIET TOWNSHEND
DAU.ER & COHEIR OF Y.E 5.TH MAR.QS

MARMION EDWARD FERRERS
LORD OF BADDESLEY CLINTON
BY RIGHT BARON DE FERRERS OF
CHARTLEY & BARON COMPTON

Special events
Typical events are Bug hunts, Easter egg trails and other family
activities – get in touch!

By the way...
- The public bridleway is also a cycle path.
- We can loan you a baby or infant sling, and we have changing
facilities.
- Level entrance and 4 wheelchairs available. Some stairs.

Berrington Hall

Historic house Garden Park

nr Leominster, Herefordshire,
HR6 0DW. 01568 615721

OPENING TIMES

House
5 Mar–20 Mar 1pm–4.30pm
Sat, Sun
21 Mar–30 Oct 1pm–4.30pm
Mon–Wed, Sat, Sun

Garden, Shop, Restaurant
5 Mar–20 Mar 12pm–5pm
Sat, Sun
21 Mar–30 Oct 12pm–5pm
Mon–Wed, Sat, Sun
5 Nov–18 Dec 12pm–4.30pm
Sat, Sun

Park walk
2 Jul–30 Oct 12pm–5pm
Mon–Wed, Sat, Sun
5 Nov–18 Dec 12pm–4.30pm
Sat, Sun

Notes
Open Good Fri. From 5 Mar to
30 Oct house access 12pm–
1pm is by guided tour only

ADMISSION PRICES
£5.00, child £2.50, family £12.50

Grounds only
£3.50

Joint ticket with Croft Castle
£6.50

Wander around inside this elegant late 18th-century house designed by Henry Holland, with its nursery, Victorian laundry and Georgian dairy. Or stroll in the equally attractive gardens designed by 'Capability' Brown, with sweeping views to the Brecon Beacons.

Dressing up
Flip through this book to the page on Snowshill Manor, and you'll realise why Charles Wade didn't have room for his costume collection there. A lot of it is housed here instead, and some is always on display.

What to see
- Two commodes in the very elegant white and gold drawing room (not very private!)
- Dolls and dolls' houses, and a lovely rocking chair in the Victorian nursery.
- Pet sheep in the walled garden, and peacocks parading in the grounds.

What to do
- Visit the children's play area or try out the children's quiz. Or have a go at the 'I spy' garden quiz sheet.
- Pick up a free family activity pack for exploring the house.
- Try the orienteering course, but don't lose your bearings.

Special events
Food fayres, deer park rides and carriage parades are just some of our recent events, as well as special activities during holiday times. Get in touch!

By the way...
- There's a lovely living willow tunnel in the children's play area.
- Baby-changing facilities, and baby slings for loan.
- We have wheelchairs, but should warn you that there are many steps to enter the house.

Brockhampton Estate

Historic house   Woodland   Wildlife

This fairytale medieval moated manor house has a lovely crooked gatehouse and ruined Norman chapel and is set in extensive areas of woods and traditionally farmed land. We're sure there are some tree sprites in the garden – there are certainly some fun wooden sculptures on the woodland walks.

That's a Great Hall
Inside the house you can see an immense Great Hall, open up to the rafters – and they're made from wood from the estate. Many of those ancient oaks and beeches are still standing.

What to see
- Harold the Shire – a full-size replica shire horse made from a windblown Oak.
- In the house, spot a carved wooden lion, and leather fire buckets from the 19th century.
- Sculptures showing scenes from working life in the past.

What to do
- Follow the Nursery Rhyme trail or visit the wildflower meadow.
- Take one of the waymarked walks – Ash, Holly, Beech or Oak. Dogs can come too, under strict control.
- Buy local crafts and produce from The Granary at Lower Brockhampton.

By the way...
- Wonderful place for picnics.
- Farm tours and guided walks by arrangement.
- Pushchairs admitted. Fairly accessible, but parkland can be uneven and muddy so watch out.

Greenfields, Bringsty,
Worcestershire, WR6 5TB
01885 482077

OPENING TIMES
ESTATE
All year until dusk Daily

House, Tea-room
4 Mar–26 Mar 12pm–4pm
Sat, Sun
1 Apr–30 Sep 12pm–5pm
Wed–Sun
1 Oct–29 Oct 12pm–4pm
Wed–Sun

Notes
Also open Good Friday,
12pm–5pm. NB Tea room
closes 30 mins after house

ADMISSION PRICES
House
£4.00, child £2.00, family
£10.00, groups £3.50

Calke Abbey

Ticknall, Derby, Derbyshire,
DE73 1LE. 01332 863822

OPENING TIMES

House
18 Mar–29 Oct 12.30pm–5pm
Mon–Wed, Sat, Sun

Garden & church
18 Mar–29 Oct 11am–5pm
Mon–Wed, Sat, Sun
29 Jun–1 Sep 11am–5pm Daily

Restaurant & Shop
18 Mar–29 Oct 10.30am–5pm
Mon–Wed, Sat, Sun
4 Nov–26 Nov 11am–4pm
Sat, Sun
27 Nov–17 Dec 11am–4pm
Mon–Wed, Sat, Sun
6 Jan–11 Mar 07 11am–4pm
Sat, Sun

Café/kiosk
29 Jun–1 Sep 11am–5pm
Thu–Sun

Notes
Admission by timed ticket.
Ticket office opens 11pm. Park:
Open most days until 9pm or
dusk

ADMISSION PRICES

£6.80, child £3.40, family £17.00.
Groups £5.80, child £2.90

Garden only
£4.20, child £2.10, family
£10.50

Calke was built in 1701–4 and isn't really an Abbey; for years it was
home to the eccentric Harpur Crewe family, who never threw much
away. It hasn't changed much since the l880s, and gives an amazing
glimpse of 19th-century life. It's also a magical and especially child-
friendly place, with some special trails.

Invisible servants
The owners were a funny lot – they didn't want to see their servants so
they built secret corridors and tunnels for them to use. If a servant
bumped into a member of the family, they had to turn their face to the
wall and pretend to be invisible!

What to see
- Some rather weird collections – cannonballs, shells and stones, and
  even an alligator skull.
- An aviary with pheasants in it.
- A stunning Chinese silk bed.

What to do
- See how many people you can fit into the hollow tree in the
  grounds.
- Find the secret walled garden behind a shrubby area.
- Romp around in the grounds–there's a guide to the park.

Special events
Apple day, Father Christmas and East Egg hunts have featured in the
past. Call us to find out what's on.

By the way..

- Calke is very popular, so it can take a while to get in on bank holidays.
- There are wheelchairs available. Quite a lot to see on the ground floor, stairs to the other floors.
- Ask the room steward to show you what items can be touched, or get a list from the entrance hall.
- There's no shaded parking, so think before bringing the dog.

Charlecote Park

Warwick, Warwickshire,
CV35 9ER. 01789 470277

OPENING TIMES

House
4 Mar–30 Sep 12pm–5pm
Mon, Tues, Fri–Sun
1 Oct–29 Oct 12pm–4.30pm
Mon, Tues, Fri–Sun

Park & Gardens
4 Mar–29 Oct 10.30am–6pm
Mon, Tues, Fri–Sun
4 Nov–17 Dec 11am–4pm
Sat, Sun

Restaurant
4 Mar–29 Oct 10.30am–5pm
Mon, Tues, Fri–Sun
4 Nov–17 Dec 11am–4pm
Sat, Sun

Last admission
30 mins before closing

ADMISSION PRICES
£6.90, child £3.50, family £17.00.
Groups £5.90

Grounds only
£3.50, child £1.85
Reduced rate when arriving by
public transport, cycle or on
foot. Croquet set available £3.50
per hour (deposit required)

A grand Tudor house with a landscaped deer park and a formal garden by the River Avon. It's been in the Lucy family for at least 700 years. The imposing Elizabethan gatehouse made from pink brick provides a warm welcome and the rest of the house was largely restored in the 19th century and is in 'Elizabethan Revival' style, complete with ornate ceilings and vaulting.

Deer me
A certain William Shakespeare was allegedly caught poaching in the deer park. Perhaps his plays weren't doing so well at the time. Another famous visitor – this time invited – was Queen Elizabeth I, who stayed at Charlecote for two nights in 1572.

What to see
- A fascinating collection of carriages and other vehicles.
- Look out for the Lucy family's symbol – a fish – it's all around the house.
- Elizabethan stained glass windows in the Great Hall, and a famous table covered with marbles and semi-precious stones.

What to do
- Visit the Victorian kitchen and scullery, the laundry room and the brew-house – kitted out with original equipment like washtubs and vats.
- Spot herds of red and fallow deer roaming capably in 'Capability' Brown's parkland.
- Or explore the children's maze in the play area, with carved wooden deer.

Special events
We cater well for families, and have had bat walks, kite festivals, spinning and weaving demos as well as storytelling and spooky Halloween activities. Get in touch!

By the way...
- There's a ramped entrance, and the ground floor is accessible. We've wheelchairs you can borrow.
- Baby-changing facilities, and carriers for loan, and a children's menu in the restaurant.

Chedworth Roman Villa

Roman villa   Museum

A stately home with a difference – it's over 1700 years old. Here are the remains of one of the largest Romano-British villas in the country, nestled in a beautiful wooded valley in the heart of the Cotswolds. Unlike some Roman sites, here a lot has been uncovered and you can really get a sense of how the villa would have been.

Hypo heat
Did you know that the Romans had fancy underfloor heating to keep their tootsies warm? You can still see evidence of hypocausts at Chedworth – that's special flooring that was held up by columns to let the hot air through.

What to see
* Mosaics, bath-houses, latrines (Roman loos)
* The remains of a water-shrine.
* About 1.6 kilometres (over a mile) of ancient walls.

What to do
* Follow the site trail and imagine life as a rather posh Roman
* Our audio-visual show brings the archeology to life.
* New this year – family activity packs.

Special events
There are archeological events throughout the year, and we also have special holiday activities and weekend days – like recreations of life as a gladiator (including battles) and spooky Halloween days.

By the way...
* Most of the site has steps although the entrance is ramped and we have a wheelchair.
* We have lots of 'living history' events with re-enactors to talk to and artifacts to handle.

Yanworth, nr Cheltenham, Gloucestershire, GL54 3LJ
01242 890256

Central

OPENING TIMES
Villa & Shop
1 Mar–25 Mar 11am–4pm
Tue–Sun
26 Mar–28 Oct 10am–5pm
Tue–Sun
29 Oct–12 Nov 10am–4pm
Tue–Sun

Notes
Open BH Mons

ADMISSION PRICES
£5.40, child £2.70, family £13.50
Audio tour
£1.20, child 80p

Clumber Park

Central

The Estate Office, Clumber
Park, Worksop,
Nottinghamshire, S80 3AZ
01909 476592

OPENING TIMES

Park
All year, daylight. Daily (except
8 Jul &19 Aug for concert days)

Kitchen garden
1 Apr–1 Oct 10am–6pm
Sat, Sun, 10am–5pm Mon–Fri

Shop/restaurant, plant sales
1 Apr–1 Oct 10am–6pm
Sat, Sun
3 Apr–29 Sep 10am–5pm
Mon–Fri
2 Oct–31 Mar 07 10am–4pm
Daily

Notes
Main facilities open BH Mons,
closed 25/26 Dec. Chapel open
as shop but closed 12 Jan–
31 Mar 2006 for cleaning. Cycle
hire and Information point open
as shop except Oct–Mar, when
open weekends and school
holidays only.

ADMISSION PRICES

Vehicle entry charge
£4 per car; £5.50 car +
caravan, minibus, car + trailer;
coaches free

Walled kitchen garden
£2, child free

Orienteering
By arrangement

Horse riding
By permit only

Coarse fishing
16 Jun–14 Mar; tel. for details

Clamber around Clumber and you'll find 1540 hectares (3800 acres)
of woods, open heath and rolling farmland. In the middle is a superb
serpentine lake. Formerly home to the Duke of Newcastle, the house
was demolished in 1938 but there is still a chapel and a fascinating
walled kitchen garden with some spectacular glass houses.

How many dukes does it take to change a lightbulb?
Can't help you there, but we do know that this district here was once
called 'The Dukeries' because it had the five ducal residences of the
Dukes of Newcastle, Kingston, Portland, Norfolk and Leeds.

What to see
- The longest greenhouse owned by the NT – that's 137 metres
(450 feet) long.
- The longest avenue of lime trees in Europe – that's 3 kilometres
(2 miles).
- Clumber Chapel, made as a mini Gothic cathedral – that's small.

What to do
- Bring your bike, or hire one from us (check when we're open). There
are gentle cycle routes, or longer routes for seasoned pedallers.
- Stick your hands in the feeling box in the Conservation Centre, and
grab deer antlers, animal fur and who knows what else.
- Let the dog off in the park but not the gardens or grazing
enclosures, please.

Special events
We have spider walks and teddy bears' picnics. Call for more details.

By the way...
- We have wheelchairs, and ramped entrance to the chapel and
garden.
- You can hire an adapted cycle, as well as tandems and trikes.

Dudmaston

Dudmaston takes its name from a 12th-century Knight, Hugo de Dudmaston, who was given the land here, but the house wasn't built until the late 17th century. It's a house full of art works amassed by the previous owners, Sir George and Lady Labouchère, with a significant collection of 20th-century sculpture and painting by artists like Barbara Hepworth and Henry Moore.

It all adds up
A less-known fact about Dudmaston is that it's linked with Charles Babbage, the inventor of the first computer. He married a daughter of the house in 1814 and often came to stay. Perhaps he wandered in the parkland thinking about bytes and bits – we hope he didn't come a'cropper.

What to see
- Stunning botanical paintings that show every intricate detail of plants.
- Chinese porcelain, French furniture and Spanish watercolours – these Labouchères got about a bit!
- Terraced lawns with oaks and cedars stretching down to the 'Big Pool' lake.

What to do
- Enjoy a dally in the Dingle – a wooded valley – or a walk through the flower gardens.
- See a display of Lady Labouchère's childhood clothes.
- Arrive by the Severn Valley Railway at Hampton Loads.

Special events
All sorts – garden walks, half-term Halloween, 18th-century Christmas … get in touch to see what's on.

By the way...
- Baby-changing facilities and hip-carrying sling available. Log pile for children to play on too.
- Shady area for parking with doggie on board.
- Children's menu and ice-cream kiosk too.
- There are wheelchairs and the ground floor is accessible. We've a map of accessible garden routes.

Quatt, nr Bridgnorth,
Shropshire, WV15 6QN
01746 780866

OPENING TIMES

House
2 Apr–27 Sep 2pm–5.30pm
Tue, Wed, Sun

Garden
2 Apr–27 Sep 12pm–6pm
Mon–Wed, Sun

Shop
2 Apr–27 Sep 1pm–5.30pm
Tue, Wed, Sun

Tea-room
2 Apr–27 Sep 11.30am–5.30pm
Mon–Wed, Sun

ADMISSION PRICES
£5.00, child £2.50, family
£12.50, groups £4

Garden only
£4.00, child £2.00, family £9.00

Hardwick Hall

Historic house Garden Park Farm Countryside

Doe Lea, Chesterfield,
Derbyshire S44 5QJ

OPENING TIMES

Hall
25 Mar–29 Oct 12pm–4.30pm
Wed, Thur, Sat–Sun

Garden
25 Mar–29 Oct 11pm–5.30pm
Wed–Sun

Parkland
All year 8am–6pm Daily

Shop, Restaurant
25 Mar–29 Oct 11am–5pm
Wed–Thur, Sat–Sun

Old Hall (English Heritage)
25 Mar–29 Oct 11am–1pm.
2pm–4pm, Wed–Thur, Sat–Sun
(joint tickets available)

Notes
Open BH Mons and Good Fri:
12pm–4.30pm. Parkland closes
at dusk in winter

ADMISSION PRICES

House & Garden
£7.80, child £3.90, family
£19.50

Garden only
£4.00, child £2.00, family
£10.00

Hardwick Hall is a truly spectacular Tudor house, one of the most complete in Britain. It presides over the Derbyshire with the same grandeur that its builder, Bess of Hardwick, did.

The Queen's Rival

Elizabeth Hardwick, known as Bess of Hardwick, was the second most powerful and wealthy woman in Tudor England – she rivaled Queen Elizabeth I. Ambitious in her choice of husbands, she even married off one of her daughters to Charles Stuart, brother of the late husband of Mary Queen of Scots, who had both Royal Tudor and Stuart blood in his viens. Their daughter, Arbelle Stuart, was in direct line for the throne of England.

What to see

- See how this powerful Tudor aristocrat would have lived – Hardwick remains virtually unchanged since Bess lived here.
- Learn about the rare breeds of sheep and cattle.
- See the new 'Bess' exhibition in the Butler's Pantry.
- Outstanding 16th and 17th-century tapestries and embroideries.

What to do

- Have a picnic in the stunning parkland.
- Take a walk around the Elizabethan walled courtyards, visit the orchard and spot different apple varieties.
- Take a tour of the stonemason's yard.
- There are lots of events held every year, so phone up and ask: search through the undergrowth on a Fungi Foray, dress up as a witch for Halloween and take party in the Bat Hunt or Pumpkin competition, put on a spooky costume and take a haunted tour of the house.

Kedleston Hall

Historic house   Park   Lake

A really sumptuous Palladian mansion, built between 1759 and 1765 for the Curzon family. Magnificent state rooms designed by Robert Adams, loads of paintings, a museum with weird objects from Lord Curzon's Indian travels, and walks in the restored 18th-century 'pleasure grounds' – complete with a lakes and cascades. A very grand day out with lots to enjoy.

Out of my way!
Sir Nathaniel Curzon, who inherited Kedleston in 1758, thought the village spoilt the view from where he wanted his new house to go. So he had the village moved, stone by stone. What a nerve!

What to see
- Curious trompe l'oeil paintings that can fool you into thinking they're 3-D.
- A summer house and numerous sculptures hiding in the grounds.
- A model of the Taj Mahal in the Eastern Museum.

What to do
- Count the amazing alabaster columns in the Marble Hall as you go inside the house. Then look up at that ceiling – wow!
- Look out for the grand bed decorated with ostrich feathers.
- Have a go at the children's quiz.

Special events
Contact us for details. In the past we've had children's theatre shows, spinning demonstrations and craft workshops.

By the way...
- The parkland is a great place to romp, and dogs on leads are welcome.
- There's an alternative entrance avoiding the steps, and we have wheelchairs available. The upper floor has a flight of 22 steps.
- We can loan you a hip-carrying infant seat, and there are baby-changing facilities and a children's menu in the restaurant.

Derby, Derbyshire, DE22 5JH
01332 842191

Central

OPENING TIMES

House
11 Mar–29 Oct 12pm–4.30pm
Mon–Wed, Sat, Sun

Garden
11 Mar–29 Oct 10am–6pm Daily

Park
11 Mar–29 Oct 10am–6pm Daily
30 Oct–9 Mar 07 10am–4pm Daily

Shop
11 Mar–29 Oct
11.30am–5.30pm Mon–Wed, Sat, Sun
4 Nov–4 Mar 12pm–4pm Sat, Sun

Restaurant
11 Mar–29 Oct 11am–5pm Mon–Wed, Sat, Sun
27 Jul–1 Sep 12pm–4pm Thu–Fri
4 Nov–4 Mar 12pm–4pm Sat, Sun

Church
11 Mar–29 Oct 11am–5pm Mon–Wed, Sat, Sun.

Last admission
30 mins before closing

Notes
Open Good Fri. Park: occasional day restrictions may apply in Dec 2006 and Jan 2007. Closed 25/26 Dec

ADMISSION PRICES
£6.90, child £3.30, family £17.00.
Groups £5.80, child £2.90

Park & garden only
£3.10, child £1.55, family £7.70. Reduced rate when arriving by public transport, cycle or on foot. (Park & garden ticket refundable against tickets for house.)

Snowshill Manor

House   Garden   Collections

Snowshill, nr Broadway,
Worcestershire, WR12 7JU
01386 852410

OPENING TIMES

House
25 Mar–29 Oct 12pm–5pm
Wed–Sun

Garden, Shop & Restaurant
25 Mar–29 Oct 11am–5.30pm
Wed–Sun, 4 Nov–10 Dec
12pm–4pm Sat, Sun (Rest &
shop)

Notes
Admission by timed ticket
which cannot be pre-booked.
On busy days house tickets run
out, so please arrive early to
avoid disappointment. Open
BH Mons

ADMISSION PRICES

**Garden, restaurant/shop
only**
£4.00, child £2.00, family £10.00

House & garden
£7.30, child £3.65 family £18.50.
Visitors arriving by bicycle or on
foot offered a voucher for the
shop or tea-room

The house of architect and craftsman Charles Paget Wade, who was
a passionate collector. There are over 5000 objects to peruse, from
Samurai warriors to spinners' tools. The organic garden is just as
eccentric, with a magical combination of terraces and ponds forming
little outdoor rooms.

Crowded house
Charles just didn't know when to stop – he started collecting at age 7,
and by 1919 he had so much stuff in this house that he had to move
next door. Have you ever wished you could do that?

What to see
- Musical instruments, clocks, toys, masks,
- Samurai armour, Wade's great-great-grandmothers' barrel organ
- Bicycles in the room of One Hundred Wheels.
- Model ships in every spare space. And that's just for starters…

What to do
- Explore the rooms each named by Wade to reflect what is in them –
  our favourite: Seventh Heaven and Dragon.
- Pick up a children's discovery sheet and explore the garden, or a
  quiz sheet in the house.

Special events
Check with us – we've had a Neptune treasure hunt, an Easter bunny trail, Ugly Bug Ball, plus Samurai martial arts groups fighting on the lawn. Who knows what might be on the cards…

By the way…
- Baby-changing facilities. We can loan a baby sling or carrier.
- Please don't take photos without written agreement – ask us first.
- It's a 10-minute walk to the house along a bumpy path. Once inside, we have 2 wheelchairs. Touchable objects and interesting sounds – ask about our handling collection.

MILLS, MEN & MARVELLOUS MACHINES

How about a visit to an example of Britain's amazing industrial heritage? The National Trust cares for a broad range of industrial sites and buildings, together with the machinery inside them. They're a fascinating way to learn more about Britain's industrial past, and a real eye-opener for all members of the family. Often there's a chance to try things 'hands-on' and to see industrial machinery in action.

Quarry Bank Mill in Cheshire has working machinery, and a unique insight into the lives of pauper child workers. The Wellbrook Beetling Mill in Country Tyrone is another example of a textile mill, and still produces calico, which is for sale in the shop. Right in the middle of town the Winchester City Mill in Hampshire has hand-milling of flour, and you can often join in.

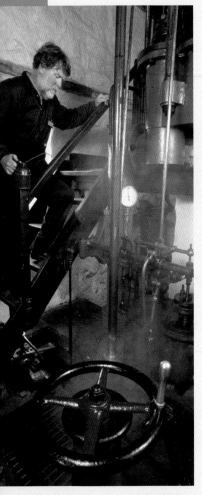

While we're talking water power, visit Cragside, the home of eccentric 19th-century inventor and engineer, William Armstrong. He used it to power his lifts, lighting and central heating, not to mention his loos! (Please phone for more details, as Cragside is being refurbished in 2006.) Then there's Patterson's Spade Mill in Templepatrick, Northern Ireland, the last surviving water-driven spade mill in Ireland – and still making spades today – and the Finch Foundry in Devon, where you can often see demonstrations of the machinery in action.

If you haven't got water power, then wind power's a fashionable choice! Just to show that there's nothing new under the sun, visit some of the many windmills in Britain at Pitstone Windmill in Buckinghamshire, Bembridge Windmill on the Isle of Wight or the wonderfully named Horsey Windpump, in Norfolk.

In fact the lists of mills, both water and wind-powered, is so long that we'll just list a few others here: Houghton Mill in Cambridgeshire, Nether Alderley Mill in Cheshire, Stainsby Mill in Derbyshire, Bourne Mill in Essex and Dunster Working Watermill and Stembridge Tower Mill in Somerset. You can pretty much guarantee that where there's some windswept countryside or a rolling river, a mill was built to take advantage of all that free power!

Mining has always been a feature of Britain's past, and you can see powerful reminders at Aberdulais Falls in Wales – complete with water wheel and hydroelectrics – and the Dolaucathi Gold Mines in Carmarthenshire. Not much gold there now, but it's nice to dream! The Cornish Mines and Engines are partly restored to working condition, and remind us of Cornwall's important mining history. You can see a giant 27-metre (90-foot) beam engine and visit a fascinating Industrial Discovery Centre to learn more. In Cumbria, the Force Crag Mine in Borrowdale was the last working mineral mine in the Lake District, and the buildings and machinery

have been restored (it's very remote, so telephone to check when we're open!).

While no man is an island, so they say, Britain is. That means that coastal defences have always been important, since early times. The same building and mechanical innovations that brought mills and mining, also provided better military protection. On the Isle of Wight you can marvel at the original cannon at the **Needles Old Battery**, and explore the fascinating military history, or in East Anglia admire the **Martello Tower** at **Orford Ness**, built against a potential Napoleonic invasion. Orford Ness has a long military history through both World Wars, so if that's your interest you'll enjoy the many military buildings and exhibitions here. (Of course, fortifications and defences go back a long way to pre-industrial times – take a brisk Northumbrian walk along **Hadrian's Wall** and visit **Houstead's Fort** to see how the Roman's did it. And don't forget our feature on castles.)

Visit the National Trust website at **www.nationaltrust.org.uk** to find more information about the many other industrial and commercial buildings owned by the National Trust.

Shugborough Estate

Historic house   Farm   Walks

Milford, nr Stafford,
Staffordshire, ST17 0XB
01889 881388

OPENING TIMES

House
17 Mar–27 Oct 11am–5pm
Daily

**Servants' Quarters,
Parkland, & Tea-room**
As for house

Shop
17 Mar–27 Oct 11am–5pm
Daily
28 Oct–23 Dec 11am–4pm
Daily

Notes
Opening times may vary when
special events held. Tel. or see
website for details.

ADMISSION PRICES

NT members (free entry to
house gardens only)

All sites ticket
£6.00, family £15.00

Non-members/day visitors:
£10.00, child £6.00, family
£25.00, concessions £7.00
Visitors may return to visit sites
not seen on day of ticket

Shugborough is extremely family-friendly with loads going on. This elegant 17th-century mansion is the home of Lord Lichfield, better know as the photographer Patrick Lichfield. There's a working kitchen and laundry, and a brewery nearby. In the parkland there's a Rare Breed farm with working watermill, kitchens and dairy – and animals of course. The gardens have a unique collection of unusual monuments and a lake.

Ahhhh!

The farm at Shugborough has been going since 1805 and is home to some rare breed farm animals, like Snowdrop the miniature Dexter cow. Her baby calf was only 30 centimetres (12 inches) tall when he was born!

What to see

- A working kitchen and laundry – come face to face with our characters from the past in an historic reconstruction.
- A working dairy – with cheese-making!
- Sheep on the drive in, and rare breed animals and poultry on the farm.

What to do

- Have a go on the children's adventure playground, and climb aboard Lucy the train for a free ride from the ticket office to the farm.
- Try and crack the code under the 'Shepherds' monument in the grounds. Nobody has yet!
- Watch the working historic watermill in action.

Special events

So many! The whole experience is very interactive. We have events *every day* during the school holidays!

By the way...

- There are wheelchairs available, and a ramped entrance. Some steps to the upper floors and elsewhere.
- Call first, and we'll arrange touchable objects for you to try.
- Baby-changing and feeding facilities, children's menu and hip-carrying child slings all available. Push-chairs ok at the farm.

Sudbury Hall

National Trust Museum of Childhood   Historic house   Garden

The Museum of childhood is the ideal place to visit on a soggy day when you'd rather be inside. Loads of hands-on activities for children of all ages, and if it clears up the lake is a great spot for picnics and games. The Hall dates back to the late 17th century, and the interiors are very opulent – they were the setting for the BBC's *Pride & Prejudice*.

For kids of all ages

The museum is housed in the 19th-century service wing, and has fascinating displays about children from the 18th century onwards. Smaller (and pluckier) members of the family can try a chimney sweep climb, and there are all sorts of buttons and switches you can try to make toy engines work and signs light up.

What to see

- In the hall, snaffle an 'I-Spy' sheet to help you spot shapes and pictures of grasshoppers, crayfish and other animals.
- Gawp at one of the grandest staircases in England.
- In the museum, a Victorian schoolroom (you can even take 'lessons' there).

Sudbury Hall, Ashbourne, Derbyshire, DE6 5HT Museum 01283 585337

OPENING TIMES
Museum & Hall
6 Mar–29 Oct 1pm–5pm
Wed–Sun (22 Jul–2 Sep
Museum open daily)
Grounds: 11 Mar–29 Oct
11am–6pm Wed–Sun

Tea–room & shop

11 Mar–21 Jul 11am–5pm
Wed–Sun
22 Jul–2 Sep 11am–5pm Daily
3 Sep–29 Oct 11am–5pm
Wed–Sun
(shop opens same dates as
tea–room but 12.30pm–5pm)

Museum
Tea-room: 6 Mar–30 Oct
11.30am–5pm Wed–Sun
3 Dec–11 Dec 11am–4pm
Sat, Sun
Shop: 6 Mar–30 Oct
12.30pm–5pm Wed–Sun
3 Dec–11 Dec 11am–4pm
Sat, Sun

Notes
Museum & Hall open BH Mons

ADMISSION PRICES (peak prices apply during school holidays, tel. for details)
Hall (standard tariff)
£5.50, child £2.50, family £13.00.
Joint ticket for Hall & Museum
£10.00, child £5.50, family £25.00
Garden only £1.00, child 50p,
family £2.50
Museum
£5.50, child £3.50, family £12.50.
Joint ticket for Hall & Museum:
£9.00, child £4.50, family £20.00
Reduced rate when arriving by
public transport or cycle

continued…   101

What to do

- In the hall, uncover life 'below stairs' with our Meet the Butler tours.
- Or encounter smells (and feels) of the past in special treasure chests.
- In the museum, younger visitors can choose a teddy bear to accompany them round the Museum – no, not you Dad …
- … though you could make yourself tiny with a trip down the 'shrinking corridor'.

Special events

We have all manner of events in the holidays, and sometimes the chance to try on period costume, or have a go at tapestry. Call us.

By the way...

- Avoid a dull day if you want to see the paintings clearly; we don't have very bright lighting.
- Kids have to be accompanied around the museum, by grown-up kids.
- The steps to the nursery area are very tiny, but otherwise pretty accessible.

The Workhouse

Historic building   Gardens

The Workhouse is the least altered example of a kind of 'welfare' brought about by the New Poor Law of 1834. Paupers – poor people who had no work, or had fallen into debt or disgrace – lived in grim conditions here. It's worth a visit to see just how life has changed.

Or has it?
You can see a full recreated 19th-century dormitory with replica beds here. But next door there is also a recreation of a bedsit, to remind you that the building's most recent welfare use was as housing for the temporarily homeless in the '70s.

What to see
A film to start with, where the Reverend Becher will introduce the Workhouse and bring it to life.
The old workshops and dormitories.
Segregated rooms for women and men – and segregated stairways too!

What to do
Follow the excellent audio guide, which is based on archive records and brings the building to life.
Interact with displays that tell you about poverty through the years.
Play 'The Master's Punishment' game.

Upton Road, Southwell, Nottinghamshire, NG25 0PT
01636 817250

OPENING TIMES
25 Mar–9 Apr 12pm–5pm Sat–Sun
10 Apr–23 Apr 12pm–5pm Mon, Wed–Sun
27 Apr–30 Jul 12pm–5pm Thur–Sun
31 Jul–1 Sep 12pm–5pm Mon, Thur–Sun

Notes
Open BH Mons and Good Fri 11am–5pm. Last admission 1hr before closing. Guided tours 31 Jul–1 Sep for a small charge

ADMISSION PRICES
£4.90, child £2.40, family £12.20. Reduced rate when arriving by public transport, cycle or on foot. Introductory video, displays and audio guide included

continued... 103

Special events

We have quite a few events, including storytelling about the goings on in the Workhouse and Halloween Crafts. Call to find out what's on when you plan to visit – you can also book in advance (free) to visit The Workhouse – a good idea at busy periods.

By the way...

- There's food in the local villages, but no café on site (it's a very authentic Workhouse!) although you can picnic here.
- Baby-changing facilities and pushchairs are fine, though you can borrow a hip-carrying infant seat.
- Get in touch if you would like to use one of our wheelchairs. It's not suitable for motorised wheelchairs.

Beatrix Potter Gallery

Here you'll find a fascinating exhibition on the life of children's author Beatrix Potter, including original illustrations for her books. It's housed inside a 17th-century Lakeland town house that was the model for Tabitha Twitchitt's shop and was once the office of Beatrix's husband, William Heelis.

Hill Top House
The house where Beatrix wrote many of her stories, left much as it was when she lived in it. There's something from one of her books in each room – see if you can spot them.

Animal tails
Characters in Beatrix Potter's books like Peter Rabbit and Tom Kitten are based on pets she had as a child. Beatrix had quite a lonely childhood, and was taught at home by a governess, but had many animal friends to keep her company.

What to see
Watercolours and sketches that Beatrix Potter drew to illustrate her books.
The lovely Lakeland countryside that inspired her.
The house she lived in.

Gallery: Main Street, Hawkshead, Cumbria, LA22 0NS
015394 36355

Hill Top: Near Sawrey, Hawkshead, Ambleside, Cumbria, LA22 0LF
015394 36269

North West

OPENING TIMES
Gallery
1 Apr–2 Aug 10.30am–4.30pm Mon–Wed, Sat, Sun
3 Aug–31 Aug 10.30am–4.30pm Mon–Thur, Sat, Sun
1 Sept–22 Oct 10.30am–4.30 pm Mon–Wed, Sat, Sun
23 Oct–29 Oct 10.30am–4.30pm Daily

Shop
4 Mar–26 Mar 10am–4pm Sat, Sun.
1 Apr–12 Nov 10.30am–4.30pm Daily
18 Nov–17 Dec 10.30am–4pm Sat, Sun
17 Feb–24 Feb 07 10.30am–4pm Daily

Notes
Admission by timed ticket issued on arrival to all visitors. Open Good Fri. Opens Thurs ! June. Shop is open occasional extra days in winter. Please enquire before making a special journey.

ADMISSION PRICES
£3.60, child £1.80, family £9. Discount available to Hill Top ticket holders (not applicable to groups)

continued...

What to do
Pick up a leaflet and take a walk around Beatrix Potter country.
Try the children's quizzes and get a goodie bag from the gallery.

Special events
At the gallery we have occasional story reading for families, and special exhibitions.

By the way...
Sorry, no toilet at the gallery. But there's one nearby in the town car park.
You do need to manage a flight of stairs to get to the upstairs gallery.
The house can get extremely busy at holiday times, and sometimes you may not be able to get in if we're full.

Dunham Massey

Outside it's an early Georgian house, built around a Tudor core. Inside, it's a wonderful example of sumptuous Edwardian interior décor, with fascinating servants' quarters. The deer park has beautiful avenues and ponds, and a newly restored Tudor mill in working order. The garden is charming and has an orangery to explore.

Motte or not?
There's a flattened mound in the garden which might be the remains of a Norman motte – an extremely old castle. An 18th-century painting of a bird's-eye view of the garden shows it clearly visible – but rather dressed up, with terraces cut into it and a gilded urn on top.

What to see
A huge collection of Huguenot silver – the finest in Britain.
A bark-house and a well-house in the garden.
The mill; originally it ground corn but now it's a sawmill.

What to do
Spot the tower and the sundial.
Pick up a childrens' quiz/trail.
Eat your sandwiches in our extensive picnic area – but not in the deer park, please!

Special events
We have family tours and activities and special family activities in the holidays. At Christmas and other times you can experience the hustle and bustle of a Victorian kitchen, or meet the butler face to face – so mind your Ps and Qs! Give us a call for more details.

By the way...
There are many touchable things, and wonderful scents and sounds in the gardens.
Although there are a lot of stairs, we do have wheelchairs.
Baby-changing, child-carrier loan and children's menu available.

Altrincham, Cheshire,
WA14 4SJ. 0161 941 1025

OPENING TIMES
House
25 Mar–29 Oct 12pm–5pm
Mon–Wed, Sat, Sun

Garden
25 Mar–29 Oct 11pm–5.30pm
Daily

Park
25 Mar–29 Oct 9am–7.30pm
Daily
30 Oct–31 Mar 07 9am–5pm
Daily

Restaurant
25 Mar–29 Oct 10.30am–5pm
Daily
30 Oct–31 Mar 07
10.30am–4pm Daily

Shop
As restaurant

Mill
25 Mar–29 Oct 12pm–4pm
Mon–Wed, Sat, Sun

Notes
Open Good Fri. Christmas gifts and lunches available Nov & Dec

ADMISSION PRICES
House & garden
£6.50, child £3.25, family £16.25. Groups £5

House or garden only
£4.50, child £2.25. Reduced rate when arriving by public transport

Fell Foot Park

Park Lake Boats Adventure playground

Newby Bridge, Ulverston,
Cumbria, LA12 8NN
015395 31273

OPENING TIMES
Open all year. 9am–5pm Daily

Shop
25 Mar–29 Oct 11am–5pm
Daily

Tea-room
As shop

Notes
Site closed 25 & 26 Dec.
Closes dusk if earlier. Facilities,
eg rowing boat hire (buoyancy
aids available), 29 Mar–30 Oct:
daily 11am–4pm (last boat),
must be returned by 4.30pm

ADMISSION PRICES
Admission free. Donations
welcome

These wonderful gardens on the shores of Lake Windermere are open all year round. They don't cost a penny to visit, and are a great place for a family afternoon out. You can paddle and swim safely, hire rowing boats to splash about in, or take a ferry to Lakeside Pier. Or you can sit back with your picnic and enjoy the view of the Lakeland fells. Sounds OK!

Fell like a bit of history?
Fell Foot Park was once the garden of a big house that has now been demolished. The National Trust is gradually restoring the park to be how it was in Victorian times.

What to see
Go on a (pushchair-friendly) walk to identify monkey puzzle and giant redwood trees. Pick up a leaflet.
Pleasure boats going by on Lake Windemere.

What to do
Hire a rowing boat – and don't drop the oars!
Spend the whole day here, swimming and picnicking.
Go mad on the huge adventure playground, with a special bit for children under seven.

Special events
We've had medieval events, with archery and mock battles, and Easter Egg hunts. Give us a call to see what's on.

By the way...
Always supervise kids while swimming and watch out for danger warnings. No launching or landing of speedboats or jet-skis.
There are staff-driven vehicles during the season, to help the less able get about.
Trusty the Hedgehog lunch boxes in the licensed tea-rooms.

Formby

There are some very friendly red squirrels here; they may even scamper up close to you in the woods. The other main attraction is the super beach, with oodles of sand, dunes and pine trees. It's a very nice and safe place that all the family can enjoy.

Squirrel these facts away...

Did you know that the red squirrel is native to Britain, but is being forced out of its natural habitat by the strong American Grey Squirrel? Red squirrels have sharp ears and a very bushy tail, which they use to steer when they're leaping in the air. They squirrel their food away for the winter, and you can see them sniffing the ground to find it again later.

What to see

Rare red squirrels chasing each other up and down the tall pine trees.
At low tide search for Neolithic elk footprints on the baked hard mud on the beach – they're few and far between, so make some of your own in the sand as well!
Wading birds on the shore, like oystercatchers and sanderlings.

What to do

Sit very still and a squirrel might feed out of your hand (bring some nibbles, or get some peanuts from the kiosk).
Have a paddle in the sea – but please be considerate of the birds who call it home.
Have a picnic sheltered in the dunes – bring your own grub, and buy an ice-cream from the van.

Special events

You can help out with our beach clean or come and learn about coastal pinewoods. There are other family-friendly events during the year – phone us for details or see the notice-board.

By the way...

The beach access has steep sand dunes, not good for people with mobility difficulties.
Baby-changing facilities. Picnic areas – no barbecues, please.
A good dog-walking place, but please keep the pooch on the lead in the squirrel walks.

Victoria Road, Freshfield,
Formby, Liverpool, L37 1LJ
01704 878591

North West

OPENING TIMES
Open all year. Dawn to dusk.

Notes
Closed 25 Dec. Property will be closed for 1 or 2 days early/mid May for resurfacing work

ADMISSION PRICES
Free.

Little Moreton Hall

Historic house   Garden

Congleton, Cheshire,
CW12 4SD. 01260 272018

OPENING TIMES

House, Shop & Restaurant
1 Mar–24 Mar 11.30am–4pm
Wed–Sun.
25 Mar–5 Nov 11.30–5pm
Wed–Sun
11 Nov–17 Dec11.30am–4pm
Sat, Sun

Notes
Open BH Mons. Access in Dec
restricted to ground floor,
garden, shop and restaurant.
Special openings at other times
for booked groups

ADMISSION PRICES
£5.50, child £2.80, family £13.
Groups £4.70, group visits
outside normal hours £10.
Special openings (inc. NT
members): £10. Reduced adult
admission rate and children
free in December.

This crooked-looking Tudor building seems to come straight out of a fairy-tale, and is Britain's most famous timber-framed manor house. Wander through the cobbled courtyard and explore the long gallery in the house, and the Elizabethan knot garden.

Oi! That's my window!
The hall has tiny windows because glass was so expensive. In fact, rich Elizabethens sometimes took their windows with them when they travelled, so that they wouldn't get pinched! In 1597 a law banned this silly behaviour.

What to see
Look in the corner of the courtyard for messages written in the woodwork by Tudor carpenters.
The buttresses round the back propping the house up – somebody didn't think before using heavy slate tiles on the Long Gallery roof.
The garderobe (a Tudor loo) sticking out over the moat. And why do you think that was … hmm?

What to do
Hunt for the sliding panel into the secret room, in the Guest's Parlour.
Chat to the fish and ducks swimming in the moat.
Have some Cheshire Cat biscuits in the restaurant.

Special events
Visit at Christmas when the house is decorated in traditional style, or scare yourselves with a spooky evening ghost tour at Halloween.

By the way...
We've a basket of touchable items, and displays that can be touched – ask us.
You can book a wheelchair, but there are stairs to upper floors.
Dogs have to stay in the car park, we're afraid.
We can loan you baby slings and infant seats. And there's a children's quiz too.

Lyme Park

Originally a Tudor house, Lyme Park was transformed into a huge Italianate palace in the 18th century, but some of the Elizabethan interiors remain. The garden has many features to explore, including a ravine garden and a conservatory. And the surrounding 570 hectares (1400 acres) of parkland is a medieval deer park.

Colin's wet shirt competition
Lyme Park's starring role came as the place where Darcy (played by actor Colin Firth) emerged from the lake in the 1995 BBC TV version of *Pride & Prejudice*. Other members of the family may be more interested in the adventure playground.

What to see
Deer in the medieval parkland, which also has an 18th-century hunting tower.
Paintings of the huge Lyme mastiff hunting dogs bred here and given as presents.
Intricate wood carvings done by Grinling Gibbons (but not of monkeys…).

What to do
Explore the moorland and woodland in the park. Dogs can come too if kept under control.
Visit The Cage, a grand garden building or 'folly' – used for watching the hunt and for banquets.
Scramble on the adventure playground.

Special events
We're especially good at weekly holiday activities, and have recently had Boredom Busters – crafts and different things to do each week – and Let's Go Fly a Kite, which speaks for itself. Call or e-mail for info.

By the way…
There's an alternative entrance to the house, avoiding steps, and we have wheelchairs. There are stairs, though.
We're very child-friendly. Baby-changing and feeding facilities, bottle-warming and slings to borrow. There's also a children's menu in the restaurant.

Disley, Stockport, Cheshire, SK12 2NX. 01663 762023

OPENING TIMES

House
27 Mar–31 Oct 1pm–5pm
Mon, Tues, Fri–Sun

Park
1 Apr–14 Oct 8am–8.30pm
Daily
15 Oct–31 Mar 07 8am–6pm
Daily

Garden
4 Mar–24 Mar 12pm–3pm
Sat, Sun
25 Mar–31 Oct 11am–5pm
Daily
4 Nov–17 Dec 12pm–3pm
Sat, Sun

Shop
25 Mar–31 Oct 11am–5pm Daily
4 Nov–17 Dec 12pm–4pm
Sat, Sun
27 Dec–1 Jan 07 12pm–4pm
Mon, Wed–Sun
6 Jan–26 Mar 12pm–4pm
Sat, Sun

Restaurant
21 Mar–30 Oct 11am–5pm
Mon, Tues, Fri–Sun

Coffee shop
See website for opening times

Notes
Open BH Mons and Good Fri 11am–5pm.

ADMISSION PRICES

House & Garden
£6.50, child £3.30, family £17.00

COUNTRYSIDE CAPERS

Devon and Cornwall has some amazing stretches of coastal countryside. For family-friendly woodland strolls, try **Heddon Valley** with stepping stones and bridges along the river, or **Plym Bridge Woods**, which is great for walks and cycle rides. Not forgetting Dartmoor National Park, with great walking in **Whiddon Deer Park** and **Fingle Bridge**.

The East of England has both open countryside and some fascinating historical sites. The **Whipsnade Tree Cathedral** in Bedfordshire is unique, or take a walk on the **Dunstable Downs**, **Wicken Fen** or in the extensive **Hatfield Forest**. In Hertfordshire there are miles of footpaths in the **Ashridge Estate** and Suffolk's 'Constable Country' has lovely pathways to **Dedham Vale**.

If you're off to the East Midlands, the **Peak District National Park** is the place to wander – we own over 12 per cent of it. Especially beautiful parts are **Dovedale**, the Longshaw Estate and the stunning drive (or walk) through **Winnats Pass**. For the brave and hardy, take in the impressive views from **Kinder Scout** (not for youngsters).

Northern Ireland is famed worldwide for its outstanding natural beauty, from the coastal paths at the foot of Ulster's highest mountain, **Slieve Donard**, to the gorse-covered Sperrin Mountains in the North. Don't forget the extraordinary **Giant's Causeway**, with extensive walks along the North Antrim Cliffs.

You're really spoilt for choice in North West Englan, with the Lake District, Cumbria, Cheshire and Merseyside to pick from. Pop over to **Helsby Hill** or **Alderly Edge**, just a stone's throw from Liverpool and Manchester. Make a Lakeland holiday of it, and explore the dunes at **Sandscale Haws**. Or move inland to **Arnside Knott** and **Holme Park Fell**, both wonderfully unspoilt areas with a wide variety of wild flowers and butterflies.

In the Lake District, explore the lovely walks through ancient forests at **White Moss Common** or be stunned by the dramatic waterfall at **Aira Force** – with all that water round, it's good to know that there are loos (as well as a tea-room) there! Consider a dip in **Tarn Hows**, a gorgeous lake with a pushchair-friendly circular walk or take a cruise across **Coniston Water**.

The South East, one of England's most densely populated areas, has quite a bit of open space. The **White Cliffs of Dover** need no introduction, but there's also **Box Hill**, **Leith Hill** and, back in Kent, 4.8 kilometres (3 miles) of the scenic **Royal Military Canal**. **The Witley Centre** is a fascinating place to find out more on the countryside and its management. Sussex offers walks over open downland at **Crowlink** and **Devil's Dyke**. And around the river Thames and the Solent, there are countryside finds like **Coombe Hill**, and the famous horse cut into the chalk escarpment at **White Horse Hill**, in Oxfordshire (while you're there, visit **Uffington Castle** and nearby **Dragon Hill** – no dragons, we're sorry to say!).

Wales has just oodles of mountain scenery and lush green valleys. How about the family friendly beaches at **Broadhaven**, **Porthdinllaen** and **Llanbedrog**, or even a chance to see dolphins at **Mwnt**? Then there are lovely summer meadow walks at **Lanlay Meadows**, freshwater lily ponds at **Bosherton** and the **Dommelynllyn Estate**, with one of Wales's most impressive waterfalls, **Rhaedr Ddu**.

Dorset, the Cotswolds and Gloucestershire have **Melbury Down**, a rich chalkland with lovely views, and **Haresfield Beacon** and **Minchinhampton** and **Rodborough Commons**. All are worth a look! A highlight for families is **Leigh Woods** in Bristol, especially if you have a pushchair to deal with. **Dyrham Park** also offers family parkland walks.

In the Midlands there's **Carding Mill Valley** and the former railway walk at the **Leak & Manifold Valley Light Railway** (don't worry, there are no trains now!). While you're in the area, enjoy the family events at **Dudmaston**, **Attingham Park** and, in particular, **Shugborough**, a working historic farm that always has a lot going on.

Last, but certainly not least, Yorkshire and the North East has amazing stretches of moorland and some of the most dramatic coastline in Britain. Explore miles of beautiful beaches, or move inland to **Wallington** or **Cragside**, both properties with extensive grounds and loads of interest for younger folks.

And that was just a few of them! Visit the National Trust website at **www.nationaltrust.org.uk** to find more information on all the other countryside areas that you can explore.

Quarry Bank Mill & Styal Estate

Mill House   Woodland walks

Styal, Wilmslow, Cheshire,
SK9 4LA. 01625 527468

OPENING TIMES

Mill, Shop
19 mar–30 Sep
10:30am–5:30pm Daily
1 Oct–18 Mar 10:30am–5pm
Tues–Sun

Apprentice House
19 Mar–30 Sep Tues–Sun
1 Oct–18 Mar Tues–Sun

Notes
Open BH Mons. Mill: last
admission 90mins before
closing. Mill open on school hol
Mons in winter. Apprentice
House open 2pm–4.30pm
weekdays, 11pm–4.30pm
weekends & school hols
(Mar–Sep); 2pm–3.30pm
weekdays, 11pm–3.30pm
weekends and school hols
(Oct–Mar). Admission to
Apprentice House by timed
ticket only, available from Mill
on arrival. Apprentice House
closed for conservation
cleaning 12–23 Dec. Site
closed 24 & 25 Dec.

ADMISSION PRICES

Mill and Apprentice House
£8, child £4.70, family £18.

Mill only
£5.50, child £3.70, family £15.
Discounted combined rail, bus
and entry tickets from within
Greater Manchester

This water-powered Georgian mill still produces cotton calico, sold in the Mill Shop. There are hands-on exhibitions and a chance to see the most powerful working waterwheel in Europe. A unique insight into Britain's industrial heritage that really brings the past to life.

Home from work
The Styal Estate is a village built especially for the people who worked at the mill. You can also visit the Apprentice House, where about 90 children who worked in the mill could live. No excuse for being late for work, then…

What to see
A long way up the main mill chimney.
The waterwheel in action – made or iron and rather large, to say the least.
Demonstrations of spinning and weaving.

What to do
Go on a tour of the Apprentice House with a costumed guide to learn what sort of conditions children who worked here had (limited during term time).
Watch the two steam engines in the mill that were used from around 1810.
Pick up a leaflet and take a walk in the woods, or picnic in the Mill meadow.

Special events
We have guided tours of the Mill at weekends at 2pm – no extra charge. Be warned that weekday mornings can be busy with educational visits from schools.

By the way…
There's a children's play area, and baby-changing and feeding facilities. Children's menu during school holidays.
The shop also has a mail order catalogue for Styal Calico.
There are hands on and interactive exhibits, and many opportunities for touching and handling objects.
There are many steps to get in, with handrail. Inside a chair lift and wheelchair is available, plus stairs with handrails inside.

Rufford Old Hall

Cor, look at all those wood beams and fancy plaster – and red brick too! This fascinating 16th-century house has a spectacular Great Hall and a fearsome collection of arms and armour. Out in the garden there are a variety of topiary displays and lots of nooks and crannies to explore – not to mention some quacking ducks on the canal.

Two's company, three's a (ghostly) crowd
Rufford is supposed to be haunted by not one but three ghosts! The 'Grey Lady', a man dressed in Elizabethan clothes, and Queen Elizabeth I – who has been seen pottering about in the dining room, but vanishes if you try to say hello. Well, how rude.

What to see
The very large Great Hall with an intricate carved screen. Some think Shakespeare acted here.
Look up to see coats of arms of the powerful local families of the time.
Wow, those 16th-century suits of armour were small – would they fit Dad?

What to do
Find the huge fireplace in the Great Hall, where a secret chamber was found–perhaps to hide Catholic priests from sight.
Enjoy the late-Victorian grounds with topiary and sculpture.
Have a picnic or enjoy a tasty snack from the Old Kitchen Restaurant.

Special events
In the past we've had magic days, a chance to stroke rescued owls, Tudor games, dancing and more. Get in touch to see what we have planned when you want to visit.

By the way...
We love kids – baby-changing facilities, slings for loan. A bottle-warming service, and Early Learning toys to play with.
Allow time; the car park can get very busy.
Tie Rover up outside the shop; we'll provide fresh water for hot dogs.
There are wheelchairs, but some steps inside. Everywhere else is pretty accessible with a bit of help from a friend.

Rufford, nr Ormskirk,
Lancashire, L40 1SG
01704 821254

OPENING TIMES
House
25 Mar–29 Oct 1pm–5pm
Mon–Wed, Sat, Sun

Garden
11 Mar–19 Mar 12pm–4pm
Sat, Sun
25 Mar–29 Oct 11am–5.30pm
Mon–Wed, Sat, Sun
1 Nov–17 Dec 12pm–4pm
Wed–Sun

Restaurant, Shop
11 Mar–19 Mar 12pm–4pm
Sat, Sun
25 Mar–29 Oct 11am–5pm
Mon–Wed, Sat, Sun
1 Nov–17 Dec 12pm–4pm
Wed–Sun

Notes
Open Good Fri. Christmas gifts and lunches available Nov–Dec

ADMISSION PRICES
£4.90, child £2.50, family £12.
Groups £3.10, child £1.30.

Garden only
£2.80, child £1.30

115

Speke Hall

Historic house   Moat   Garden

The Walk, Liverpool,
L24 1XD. 0151 427 7231

OPENING TIMES

House
22 Mar–29 Oct 1pm–5.30pm
Wed–Sun
4 Nov–3 Dec 1pm–4.30pm
Sat, Sun

Grounds
22 Mar–29 Oct 11am–5.30pm
Daily
4 Nov–21 Mar 07 11–Dusk Daily

Home Farm, Restaurant, & Shop
22 Mar–16 Jul 11am–5pm
Wed–Sun
18 Jul–10 Sep 11am–5pm
Tue–Sun
13 Sep–29 Oct 11am–5pm
Wed–Sunday
4 Nov–3 Dec 11am–4.30pm
Sat, Sun

Notes
Open BH Mons. Grounds
(garden and estate) closed
24–26 Dec, 31 Dec, 1 Jan

ADMISSION PRICES
£6.50, child £3.50, family £19.50.
Groups £5.80, child £3.20

Grounds & Home Farm only
£3.5o, child £1.80, family £10.00
Reduced rate when arriving by
cycle, on foot or by public
transport

One of the most famous Tudor manors in Britain, this rambling pile
has an atmospheric interior that covers many periods. The oldest
parts date from 1530, but there is also a fully equipped Victorian
kitchen, not to mention William Morris wallpapers in some rooms.

Only in America
There is a copy of the Hall in California, built in 1912 as a weekend
getaway by Percy T. Morgan, and designed to withstand earthquakes.
The Tudors would be proud!

What to see
- The 19th-century 'thunderbox' loo. This was supposed to be an
  improvement on the rather basic Tudor garderobes, but both
  designs 'deposit' straight into the moat … hmm.
- Adam and Eve, aka two majestic yew trees which are as old as the
  house.
- Intricately carved furniture and fancy Jacobean plasterwork.

What to do
- Search for the secret priest's hole. The Norris family, who lived here,
  were Catholics, at a time when it was against the law.
- Visit the Home Farm visitor centre, with a children's play area and
  picnic space. It was originally a 'model farm' (a small farm but with
  real animals).
- Walk through the gardens to the 'Bund', and earth bank. You can
  see Liverpool Airport – fun!

Special events
We've had Halloween mask-making and tours, Roof tours and all sorts
of summer activities. And in the summer we have a maize maze.
Contact us for more info.

By the way…
- Baby-changing facilities. We can loan a baby sling or carrier.
- Children's menu in Home Farm restaurant.
- Dogs on lead – but in the grounds only, please.
- You can book a wheelchair, and there's a vehicle to take people
  from Home Farm to the house – they're not that close together.

Beningbrough Hall & Gardens

Historic house Playground Garden

Built in 1716, this grand Georgian mansion has a dramatic exterior, and ornate Baroque interiors. The design is unusual, with a central corridor running along the whole length of the house. Outside there are interesting grounds, with a walled garden and places to picnic.

Picture perfect

In partnership with the National Gallery, Beningbrough houses over 100 famous paintings – if they're your main reason for coming, choose a bright day, as we have no electric light in most rooms. Younger visitors can also visit the DIY 'portrait room' and put themselves in the picture with the aid of mirrors, masks and 18th-century props.

What to see

A fully equipped Victorian laundry – how did posh people keep their clothes clean before the days of washing machines? Servants, of course!

Discover why bedrooms were such busy places in the 18th-century. And what it was like to live without bathrooms.

What to do

Let off steam in the brilliant wooden playground. Lots to climb around on.

Try out the quiz sheets for kids of all ages.

Explore the grounds, and look for the intriguing wooden sculptures or picnic in the walled garden.

Special events

We often have family and craft events, including Easter egg hunts and walks. Do get in touch.

By the way...

There are some cycle paths through the parkland.

Baby-changing facilities, and we can loan you a front- or hip-carrying infant seat.

The front entrance has many steps, but can help you via an alternative entrance. Wheelchairs are available on all floors, though there are stairs. Grounds have some cobbles.

Beningbrough, York, North Yorkshire, YO30 1DD
01904 470666

OPENING TIMES

House
3 Jun–28 Jun 12pm–5pm
Mon–Wed, Sat, Sun
1 Jul–1 Sep 12pm–5pm
Mon–Wed, Fri–Sun
2 Sep–29 Oct 12pm–5pm
Mon–Wed, Sat, Sun

Grounds, Shop
25 Mar–28 Jun 11am–5.30pm
Mon–Wed, Sat, Sun
1 Jul–1 Sep 11am–5.30pm
Mon–Wed, Fri–Sun
2 Sep–29 Oct 11am–5.30pm
Mon–Wed, Sat, Sun
4 Nov–17 Dec 11am–3.30pm
Sat, Sun

Restaurant
As for house 11am–5pm

Notes
Open Good Fri. Limited opening Feb 05 half-term. Tel. for details

ADMISSION PRICES

£7, child £3.20, family £16. Groups £6.50, child £4. Reduced rate when arriving by cycle

Brimham Rocks

Prehistoric rocks   Moor   Walks

Summerbridge, Harrogate,
North Yorkshire, HG3 4DW
01423 780688

OPENING TIMES
Open all year 8am–dusk Daily

Shop
18 Mar–21 May 11am–5pm
Sat, Sun
27 May–1 Oct 11am–5pm
Daily
7 Oct–29 Oct 11am–5pm
Sat, Sun
5 Nov–17 Dec 11am–dusk

Exhibition
As for shop

Kiosk (snacks and drinks)
As for shop

Notes
Facilities may close in bad
weather. Shop, kiosk and
exhibition room open daily
during local school holidays,
also BHols, 26 Dec & 1 Jan,
weather permitting

ADMISSION PRICES
Countryside free

Come and scramble on these strange and fantastic rock formations, nearly 300m (985ft) above the surrounding countryside – they're perfect for hide and seek and exploring. You'll often see more experienced rock climbers as well. The rocks were perhaps a place of ancient worship. Some have thought that Druids carved on them, but in fact the strange weathering is entirely natural.

Lovers and legends
There's a story that two young lovers leapt off a rock here because the girl's father wouldn't let them marry. As they leapt, they were miraculously saved by the wind and put down safely. It's been known as Lover's Rock ever since.

What to see
Birds nesting in the rocks, and listen out for jackdaws.
A long way – on a clear day the view is 64 kilometres (40 miles) across the countryside.
If you're lucky, rabbits, hares or even red deer.

What to do
Look for the wishing stone with a hole in it, and put your hand in to make a wish.
Pick bilberries in the summer
Count the different kinds of lichen on the rocks.

Special events
Recent events include ghostly stories and open-air children's theatre, as well as family walks. Give us a call to see what's on.

By the way...
Good footwear is a must, and wrap up warm in colder weather. In July and August it is very busy here.
Doggy has to go on a lead between April and June so that ground-nesting birds are safe.
There's a path from the car park to the main rocks; the rest is a bit rough and has slopes.

Cherryburn

The sweet little cottage was the birthplace of Thomas Bewick (1753–1828), one of Northumberland's greatest artists and wood engravers, and you can see an exhibition about him, and sometimes demonstrations of engraving and handprinting, to get a taste of how he worked. Walk along the River Tyne, where he was inspired by the wildlife and natural beauty all those years ago, and enjoy a picnic at the farm with some friendly farmyard animals to meet.

Birdman Bewick
Thomas Bewick didn't do that well at school, and left quite early on to become apprentice to an engraver, helping to engrave the designs on banknotes. But his real love was birds and wildlife, and one of his most famous books of engravings was the *Birds of Britain*. He'd have been pleased to know that the beautiful Bewick's Swan was named in his memory.

What to see
Some of Bewick's engravings, cut into wood – nowadays we can just take a photo instead!
Demonstrations of hand printing and engraving.
A secret garden with a sun dial.
Pigs, lambs and donkeys, who live in the cobbled farmyard.

What to do
Bring a picnic and enjoy it in the garden (we don't have a café, but there's plenty of room)
Pick up some prints made from Bewick's original engravings at the shop.
Take a stroll along the river.

Special Events
Recently we've had folk music and country dance in the farmyard, drawing workshops, and engraving demonstrations. Usually the cost is included in admission, and there's something going on most Sunday afternoons.

By the way...
If you contact us in advance, we can provide touchable objects and help to make your visit more accessible. There are some steps to get in and out of the building, and the farmyard is cobbled.
We can provide a Braille guide, and there's an adapted WC.

Station Bank, Mickley, nr Stocksfield, Northumberland, NE43 7DD. 01661 843276

OPENING TIMES
House and Shop
18 Mar–29 Oct 11am–5pm
Mon-Tue, Thur–Sun

Last admission
30mins before closing time

Note
Shop open at other times by arrangement

ADMISSION PRICES
£3.50, child £1.75. Groups £3.00, child £1.50

East Riddlesden Hall

Historic house   Garden   Maze   Pond

Bradford Road, Keighley, West
Yorkshire, BD20 5EL
01535 607075

OPENING TIMES

House
1 Apr–2 Jul 12pm–5pm
Tue, Wed, Sat, Sun
3 Jul–30 Aug 12pm–5pm
Mon–Wed, Sat, Sun
2 Sep–5 Nov 12pm–5pm
Tue, Wed, Sat, Sun

Shop/tea-room
1 Apr–5 Nov As house
11 Nov–17 Dec 12pm–4pm
Sat, Sun

Last admission
30mins before closing time

Notes
Open BH Mons and Good Fri.
Open additional days in school
holidays. Shop & tea-room
open (pre-booked lunches) 26
Mar (Mother's Day) 12pm–5pm

ADMISSION PRICES

£4.00, child £2.00. Groups
£3.50, child £1.80.
£1 off admission when arriving
via Keighley & District Transport
buses

This intimate 17th-century manor house is in the heart of Bronte country. Back in the 1600s, it was one of 19 (count 'em!) houses owned by wealthy royalist James Murgatroyd – an entrepreneur, who was also involved in coal mining, cloth manufacture and farming. He remodelled the house with flamboyant gothic architecture and some ornate plasterwork ceilings. In the summer, guides in authentic costume will help you to feel that you've gone back in time.

That's one hefty heifer

The Airedale Heifer is depicted in an 1830 painting at Riddlesden, and was a legendary creature in nearby Keighley. It was supposedly 3.3 metres (11 feet) long and weighed more than one and a quarter tons. People used to come from miles around to see it – now you can see a picture on the playground climbing wall.

What to see

A room with a bricked-in window so that ladies didn't have to look at the outside loo!
A 17th-century kitchen, with no mod-cons.
Intricate tapestries and embroideries that would have taken hours to make …
… which accounts for the big fireplaces and cosy wood panelling.
An enormous 17th-century oak framed barn.

What to do

Visit the Airedale Heifer playground, with swings, slides and animal rockers.
Chat to the ducks on the pond.
Explore the grass maze, also called the labyrinth.

Special events

Get in touch to see what we have on. We have spooky Halloween Activites and Christmas Carol concerts, and Easter activities for children.

By the way...

We have a handling collection of 17th-century items, and there are scented plants in the garden, as well as a Braille guide.
There are some steps, but the ground floor is accessible, and we have wheelchairs. The grounds are fully accessible and we have portable ramps. There are quite a few steps to the café.

Fountains Abbey & Studley Royal

There's so much atmosphere to soak up at this fascinating World Heritage Site. Explore the spectacular ruins of a Cistercian abbey and watermill, founded in 1132 by 13 Benedictine monks who were after a simpler life. You can also visit rooms in Fountains Hall, an Elizabethan mansion, and enjoy the Georgian water garden – one of the best surviving examples, complete with lakes, cascades and temples. There's a cute litte church and, last but not least, the medieval deer park is home to around 500 deer and other wildlife.

Woolly wealth

The monks were so busy praying that all the day-to-day labour was done by ordinary 'lay' folk. But they were quite a canny lot – the monastery was in the wool business, with sheep nibbling the rich grasslands for miles around, and the monks had quite an economic empire.

What to see

Dramatic abbey ruins with gothic arches towering above you.
The trough where the monks washed their feet – they had baths only four times a year!
Ducks and swans paddling by the statues in the water garden.
If you're lucky, a bat whizzing by your ear.

Fountains, Ripon, North Yorkshire, HG4 3DY
01765 608888

OPENING TIMES

Abbey/garden
1 Mar–31 Oct 10am–5pm Daily
1 Nov–28 Feb 10am–4pm
Mon–Thur, Sat, Sun.

Deer park
Open all year. Dawn–dusk. Daily

St Mary's Church
1 Apr–30 Sep 1pm–5pm Daily

Mill
1 Mar–31 Oct 10am–5pm Daily
1 Nov–28 Feb 10am–4pm
Mon–Thur, Sat, Sun

Shop
As for abbey

Restaurant
As for abbey

Notes
Estate open Fridays in Feb. Visitor centre restaurant closes at 4.30pm in March. Whole estate closed Fri in Nov, Dec, Jan and 24, 25 Dec. Studley Royal shop & tea room opening times vary, please check at property.

ADMISSION PRICES

£6.50, child £3.50, family £17.50. Groups £5.00, child £2.50 Groups £5.50, child £3. EH members free. Visitor centre, deer park, St Mary's Church free

Visitor centre, deer park and St Mary's Church
free

continued... 121

What to do

Spot the different temples, statues and other strange little buildings – called follies – in the gardens.

Explore the garden and find the Serpentine Tunnel, the Grotto and the Half Moon Pond.

Walk up to Anne Boleyn's seat, a folly with a wonderful 'Surprise' view.

Have a go at the quiz and trail, and see if you can identify the different kinds of deer.

Special events

In the holidays we have children's trails and craft workshops, and family tours of the Abbey, when you can dress up in monk's robes and learn more about their daily life. We occasionally have free floodlit drives through the estate for less able visitors. You need to book.

By the way...

The water gardens offer interesting sounds, and we also have a model of the Abbey in the Visitor centre, and a Braille guide.

Some areas of the grounds are less accessible, but we have maps of level routes and you can book a PMV vehicle.

There are wheelchairs available, but you need to book. There are steps (with handrails) at Fountains Hall.

Gibside

One of the North's finest landscapes, the 18th-century estate is the former home of the Queen Mother's family, the Bowes-Lyons. There are many miles of walks through woodland and by the River Derwent. Some quirky buildings, including the Column of Liberty and a Palladian chapel. Streams to paddle in, woods to explore and open spaces to run around or play a game of footie in.

We're proud of our conveniences!
We just can't hold it in – we have to tell you that our loos were judged the best in Britain by the British Toilet Association (really!) a few years ago. So, come and try out the thrones in the Queen Mum's old garden.

What to see
The estate is a Site of Special Scientific Interest – look out for red squirrels, kingfishers and other wildlife.
Not to mention hundreds of scampering rabbits.
The Liberty Column – built after the 1745 Jacobite Rebellion and taller than Nelson's (so there!).

What to do
Explore over 25 kilometres (16 miles) of woodland and riverside walks. Not all at once – pick up leaflets of routes in the info centre.
See the restored stables – not only an education centre but also still used for real horses.
Bring the dog – the grounds are a good place for walking – but on the lead, please.

Special events
Check to see if we're having any children's days coming up. At no extra charge, they include magicians, races and more.

By the way...
Some of the buildings are being restored, but there's still a lot to see.
There are baby-changing facilities and a children's menu in the tea-room.
The grounds have some steep slopes, but there's a map of an accessible route.

nr Rowlands Gill, Burnopfield,
Newcastle upon Tyne, Tyne &
Wear, NE16 6BG
01207 541820

OPENING TIMES
Grounds
6 Mar–22 Oct 10am–6pm Daily
23 Oct–4 Mar 10am–4pm Daily
Chapel
6 Mar–22 Oct 11am–4.30pm Daily
Stables
6 Mar–22 Oct 11am–4.30pm Daily
23 Oct–4 Mar 11am–3.30pm Daily
Shop/tea-room
6 Mar–22 Oct 11am–5pm Daily
23 Oct–4 Mar 11am–4pm Daily

Notes
Closed 23–26 Dec and 30 Dec–2 Jan. Last admission 6 March–22 Oct 4.30; 23 Oct–4 March 3.30. Shop & tea-room open at 10am weekends. Last entry to tea-room 15 mins before closing

ADMISSION PRICES
£5, child £3, family £15, family (one adult) £10. Groups £4.50

Hadrian's Wall & Housestead's Fort

Bardon Mill, Hexham,
Northumberland, NE47 6NN
01434 344363

OPENING TIMES

Museum/Fort and Shop
1 Apr–30 Sep 10am–6pm Daily
1 Oct–31 Mar 10am–4pm Daily

Notes
Closed 24–26 Dec & 1 Jan.
Opening times subject to
confirmation by English
Heritage. Tel. Custodian for
details

ADMISSION PRICES

Museum/Fort
£3.80, child £1.90, concessions
£2.70
Free to NT and EH members.
Hadrian's Wall, NT information
centre and shop free

A wild and evocative World Heritage site offering a taste of the Roman soldier's life – communal loos and all. The wall was built around AD 122, when the Roman Empire was at its height, and even now the ruins are impressive, and looking after the wall is a full-time job. Housteads Fort is one of the best-preserved of the sixteen forts along the Wall.

It's cold up North

Soldiers from sunnier climes were brought in to guard the Wall – the Roman name for Housesteads was Vercovicium, which means 'effective fighters'. But some of those foreign soldiers were pretty miserable up on their cold lookout posts – and you might want to bring a sweater, too.

What to see

Ruins of Roman granaries, barracks, a hospital and some of the first flushing toilets.
A model of the fort as it would have been.
Wonderful views across the countryside.

What to do

Walk like a Roman ... march along the wall, repelling imaginary Picts and Scots.

If it's a bit chilly, grab a drink and a sandwich at the kiosk, and sit inside to warm up.

Have a look in the Museum, to find out more on the history of the Wall.

By the way...

The paths are a bit uneven at Housesteads and on the wall. But there's a ramped access to the Wall at Steel Rigg.

You can drive right up to the museum.

Please keep Rover on a lead because there are sheep and ground-nesting birds nearby

A-MAZING MAZES

Pardon the pun, but some of our mazes are truly a-mazing! If you want a bit of exercise with some puzzling thrown in, then a maze is for you. And we have all kinds at our properties, from easy ground-level decorative mazes to mazes with tall hedges and complicated patterns.

Get me out of here!

Getting in and out of a maze is easier than you think. When you go in, all you have to do in order to get to the middle is to put a hand out to one side (left or right – but stick to whichever you choose!). Keep your hand on the hedge as you walk around. You mustn't lose contact – even if it leads you up a blind alley first. In a real maze, this is guaranteed to get you to the centre. And just do the process in reverse to get out again. Easy!

But remember, if you get stuck – yelling can help too!

What are mazes for?

Mazes are beautiful garden features in themselves, and were an elegant way for people to take exercise. In earlier times when meeting your boyfriend or girlfriend in private wasn't that easy – perhaps they were good places to sneak off for a cuddle! But mazes have strong historical and religious roots, too. Some are thought to be ancient symbols, and in the Middle Ages mazes were inlaid on church floors – not very hard to get out of! Some think that people followed them as a kind of worship, by walking or even kneeling as they went round in prayer.

We don't have any like that, but there's a maze made from cobbles at **Peckover House** in Cambridgeshire. Don't go around on your knees, though! It's on the site of the earlier hedge maze, and while you're there, why not hire equipment to play croquet on the lawn?

Grassy puzzles

Turf or grass mazes are simply cut into the grass, and may go back to Roman times. They may have just been to entertain people. **East Riddlesden Hall** in Yorkshire has a grass maze that's certainly fun to explore, and another maze without high hedges is the Archbishop's Maze at **Greys Court**, in Oxfordshire – no chance of getting lost, but a great brain-teaser.

Those grand mazes with hedges were all the rage in 16th-century England. National Trust properties with impressive hedge mazes include **Glendurgan Garden** in Cornwall, with a laurel maze 1 metre (3ft 4in) high (as well as the fantastic 'Giant's Stride' maypole) and Kedleston Hall in Derbyshire. At Kedleston the maze is planted from beautiful beech hedges – it's still quite young, so you may be able to peek over at the moment!

Animal amazement

Mazes are still used in science: everyone knows the maze that white mice get popped into, to try and find their way to food. We won't make you follow a maze to get to your lunch, but our maze at **Charlecote Park** in Warwickshire has some deer – of the carved wood variety.

And, finally – it's even more a-Maize-ing!

Sorry, we just couldn't help that pun to finish with. But do try out the big maize maze at **Speke Hall**, near Liverpool – it's only there in the summer and is very impressive. Not sure what happens to all the maize afterwards, but perhaps you liked our corn-y jokes about it.

See National Trust web page **www.nationaltrust.org.uk** and other entries in this book for more information on opening times and admission.

Charlecote Park
Warwick, Warwickshire,
CV35 9ER

East Riddlesden Hall
Bradford Road, Keighley,
West Yorkshire, BD20 5EL

Glendurgan Garden
Mawnan Smith, nr Falmouth,
Cornwall, TR11 5JZ

Greys Court
Rotherfield Greys,
Henley-on-Thames,
Oxfordshire, RG9 4PG

Kedleston Hall
Derby, Derbyshire, DE22 5JH

Peckover House & Garden
North Brink, Wisbech,
Cambridgeshire, PE13 1JR

Speke Hall, Garden & Estate
The Walk, Liverpool, L24 1XD

Hardcastle Crags

Woodland valleys · Walks

Estate Office, Hollin Hall,
Crimsworth Dean, Hebden
Bridge, West Yorkshire,
HX7 7AP. 01422 844518

OPENING TIMES

Hardcastle Crags
All year. Daily

Gibson Mill
1 Apr–31 Oct 11am–4.30pm
Sat, Sun

Notes
Open during school holidays,
please phone ahead for
opening times.

ADMISSION PRICES

Gibson Mill
£3, child £1.50, family £7.50.
Groups £2, child £1.20.
Reduced rate when arriving by
public transport

This beautiful woodland valley is tranquil and unspoilt. Come on foot if you can – the parking area gets very busy – and potter about near the trickling streams, or listen out for the drumming of woodpeckers.

ANTastic!

The Crags are home to the northern hairy wood ant – they don't sting, but do look a bit fearsome with their mini-pincers and have a habit of spraying you with formic acid if they get cross. So, don't get too close – and don't ask them to shave their legs!

What to see

Deep rocky ravines, tumbling streams and the millstone grit Crags.
Huge anthills, made by our hairy ant-y friends.
Gibson Mill – an 18th-century cotton mill that's being restored.

What to do

Try one of our way-marked walks, the easier 'Slurring Rock Saunter' or the more energetic 'Crags Constitutional'.
Or try our special sensory trail, with clues as to what's good to touch, smell or listen too, as well as look at
Let your dog enjoy a scramble, too.

Special events

You can book a guided walk or a special orienteering course, and there's a BSL Interpreter at all our programmed events. We've had prehistoric survival days for older kids, and bat walks and dawn chorus. Give us a call.

By the way...

Parking is limited and there is congestion during busy times. Come by bus!
Disabled parking is possible, but ask if you want to park at Gibson Mill.
Picnicking is possible.

Lindisfarne Castle

Lindisfarne Castle sits dramatically on a rocky crag on Holy Island, looking out over the Northumberland coast. Once the island was the home of an early monastery, but Viking raids forced the monks off. You reach it by driving across a 5-kilometre (3-mile) causeway, which is great fun (but only at low tide!).

An Englishman's home is his castle

The castle was originally a Tudor fort, but in 1903 it was converted into a private house for a friend by the young Edwin Lutyens. He added very typical touches like arched windows and medieval ceilings.

What to see

- The remains of the portcullis from the original fort.
- A warren of tiny rooms in the house, with lots of interesting nooks and crannies.
- The remains of St Cuthbert's Priory, built in 1082.

What to do

- Tramp up and down the windy battlements – but don't get blown away!
- Visit the walled garden designed by Gertrude Jekyll.
- Enjoy a cup of tea at Holy Island village.

By the way...

- No large packs or pushchairs allowed in the castle, and the island is steep. Flat shoes advised!
- To avoid disappointment, check safe crossing times before making a long journey – the causeway closes 2 hours before high tide until 3 hours after.

Holy Island, Berwick-upon-Tweed, Northumberland, TD15 2SH. 01289 389244

OPENING TIMES

Castle
18 Feb–26 Feb Times vary Daily
18 Mar–29 Oct Times vary Tues–Sun
26 Dec–29 Dec Times vary Tues–Fri

Garden
Open all year 10am–dusk Daily

Notes
Open BH Mons (inc. Scottish BHols). Lindisfarne is a tidal island accessed via a 5-kim (3-mile) causeway at low tide. Therefore the castle opening times vary depending on the tides. The castle will open for 4½ hrs, always including 12pm–3pm. It will open either 10.30am–3pm or 12pm–4.30pm

ADMISSION PRICES
£5.20, child £2.60, family £13

Garden only
£1.00, child free

Nostell Priory

Doncaster Road, Nostell,
nr Wakefield, West Yorkshire,
WF4 1QE. 01924 863892

OPENING TIMES

House
1 Apr–5 Nov 1pm–5pm
Wed–Sun
9 Dec–17 Dec 12pm–4pm Daily

Grounds
13 Feb–19 Feb 11am–4pm
Daily
4 Mar–26 Mar 11am–5pm Sat,
Sun
1 Apr–5 Nov 11am–6pm
Wed–Sun

Shop, tea-room
As for grounds

Park
All year 9am–5pm Daily

Notes
Open BH Mons (House 1pm–
5pm; gardens, shop & tea-
room 11am–5.30pm; park
closes dusk if earlier). Rose
garden may be closed on
occasions for private functions

ADMISSION PRICES
£6.50, child £3.25, family £16.
Groups £6

Garden only
£4, child £1.75

Plenty for the family to do in the landscaped grounds of this
magnificent 18th-century house, built on the site of an original
medieval priory in 1733. There are paintings by Breughel and
Holbein, and probably the finest collection of Chippendale furniture
in the world. It's like a really good episode of Antiques Roadshow!

A world in miniature
Peek inside the magical 18th-century dolls' house, which is 2 metres
(6 feet) high. There's a mini-leather dog, an ivory mouse, and a dining
table all laid out with teeny-weeny cutlery and silver plates. Try and spot
the difference in the way the figures of the family and the servants were
made.

What to see
Pets' graves in the rose garden and sheep in the park.
Child-sized Chippendale chairs – sorry, you can't sit on them!
A clock made by John Harrison, with workings inside made of wood.

What to do
In the gardens, find the Obelisk Lodge in the shape of a pyramid.
Burn off some energy in the adventure playground, or watch the kids
doing that from the tea-room.
Walk around the lake and say hi to the ducks.

Special events
We have family croquet and and a giant chess set in the garden. Every
summer there's a country fair with entertainment for all ages, and we've
had spooky Halloween evenings as well. Get in touch to see what's on
this year.

By the way...
With advance notice, we can provide a lot of touchable objects and
surfaces.
Wheelchairs can be booked, a lift is available to upper floors.
There are baby-changing and feeding facilities, and we can loan you
baby slings and infant carriers (sorry, no pushchairs allowed in the
house).

Nunnington Hall

Historic house Garden

This 17th-century stone house on the banks of the River Rye has some fascinating surprises. Creep up one of the three staircases to the nursery and the haunted room. And in the attics you'll discover the Carlisle collection of miniature rooms – with everything from titchy musical instruments to miniscule files and sandpaper in the carpenter's shop.

Spooky story
People say that the panelled bedroom is haunted by a spooky lady ghost who can fly through the 400-year old wooden walls.

What to see
That amazing collection of tiny objects and houses.
Needlework samplers made by young girls in the 19th century.
And watch out for the ghost!

What to do
Find out why the tea caddy in the drawing room has a lock on it.
Look out for the stuffed animal heads and skins collected on expeditions to India and Africa.
Watch the peacocks strut their stuff in the riverside walled garden.

By the way...
There are picnic tables in the tea garden, as well as a children's menu.
We can loan you infant seats and toddler reins, and there are baby-changing facilities.
It's fairly accessible, and we have wheelchairs and can provide assistance. Dogs in the car park only, please, but we have shaded parking.

Nunnington, nr York, North Yorkshire, YO62 5UY
01439 748283

OPENING TIMES
House
18 Mar–30 Apr 1.30pm–5pm Wed–Sun
3 May–31 May 1.30pm–5.30pm Wed–Sun
1 Jun–31 Aug 1.30pm–5.30pm Tues–Sun
1 Sep–30 Sep 1.30pm–5.30pm Wed–Sun
1 Oct–5 Nov 1.30pm–5pm Wed–Sun

Garden, Restaurant, Shop
As house, opens 12.30pm

Notes
Open BH Mons

ADMISSION PRICES
£5.20, child £2.60, family £13. Groups £4.70

Garden only
£2.60

North East

QUEEN ANNE DRAWING ROOM

Ormesby Hall

Historic house   Model railway   Walks

Ormesby, Middlesbrough,
TS7 9AS. 01642 324188

OPENING TIMES

House
1 Apr–29 Oct 1.30pm–5pm
Sat, Sun

Tea-room
As for house

ADMISSION PRICES
£4, child £2.50, family £10.50.
Groups £3.50

The large model railway exhibition is the main family attraction at this charming 18th-century Palladian mansion. The particularly large selection of homemade cakes in the tearoom might appeal to others in the family!

Training wheels (and buttons)
Lots of buttons to push in the 'Friends of Thomas' model railway, and watch the larger model railway, with lifelike models of the old trains *Corfe Castle* and *Pilmorr.* There are footstools for shorter enthusiasts to stand on, so that nobody misses the action.

What to see
A sun dial in the rose garden. See if you can figure out what time it is (not much hope if it's raining, though!)
The stable block, home to horses belonging to the Cleveland Mounted Police.
A Victorian laundry and kitchen.

What to do
Have a go at the children's house quiz, with I-Spy questions for younger folks. We have a family activity pack too.
Go to the Old Wing to catch those trains.
Take a circular walk through the woods and come back for tea.

Special events
There are family-friendly events nearly every month. Other events have included birds of prey, walks to collect seeds and fungus, and a Haunted House afternoon – our very scary famous Halloween activities.

By the way...
There's a children's menu in the tea-room, and we can loan baby slings and provide baby-changing facilities.
The entrance is ramped and we have wheelchairs.
If you give us notice, we can often provide a 'touchable objects' guided tour with trained guides.

Wallington

Don't be fooled by the plain exterior of this 17th-century house, home to many generations of the Blackett and Trevelyan families. Inside there's oodles of fancy plasterwork, gorgeous Pre-Raphaelite paintings and many fascinating objects. Outside there's a fabulous garden with sculptures, water features and even a wildlife hide.

The mole's revenge

Did you know that King William III died when his horse tripped over a mole hill? He'd taken the horse from Sir John Fenwick, who owned Wallington and had been executed for trying to assassinate the King. Jacobite supporters – enemies of William – used to drink a toast to the mole, or 'the little black velvet gentleman', for doing them a favour!

What to see

A stuffed porcupine fish and other oddities in the Cabinet of Curiosities begun by the wife of the 5th Baronet, in 1791.
A collection of dolls' houses in the servants' quarters. Peep through two keyholes and a mouse hole to see the mouse house.
Some very large stone Griffin heads on the lawn – like something out of Harry Potter!

Cambo, Morpeth,
Northumberland, NE61 4AR
01670 773600

OPENING TIMES

House
5 Apr–3 Sep 1pm–5.30pm
Mon, Wed–Sun
4 Sep–29 Oct 1pm–4.30pm
Mon, Wed–Sun

Walled garden
1 Apr–30 Sep 10am–7pm Daily
1 Oct–31 Oct 10am–6pm Daily
1 Nov–31 Mar 10am–4pm Daily

Shop & Retaurant
1 Mar–28 May 10.30am–5.30pm
Mon, Wed–Sun
29 May–3 Sep 10.30am–5.30pm
Daily
4 Sep–29 Oct 10.30am–4.30pm
Mon, Wed–Sun
1 Nov–11 Feb 10.30am–4.30
Wed–Sun
12 Feb–26 Mar 10.30–5.30pm
Mon, Wed–Sun

Grounds
All year Dawn–dusk Daily

Last admission
Shop and restaurant closed 20 Dec–13 Jan inc. Farm Shop (outside the turnstile) closed 25–27 Dec & 1–2 Jan 06. Gardens open all year except 25 Dec

ADMISSION PRICES

House, garden & grounds
£8, child £4, family £20. Groups £6.80

Garden & grounds only
£5.50, child £2.75, family £14. Groups £4.70

continued...

133

What to do
Visit the children's room (no adults allowed!) filled with old-fashioned games and toys.
Have a clamber around in the adventure playground.
Imagine doing loads of washing-up in that kitchen without a dishwasher!

Special events
We have quite a few family-friendly activities. Recent events have included Rupert Bear's tea party, Halloween escapades and lots more. Get in touch!

By the way...
There are lots of small objects, so we do encourage babies to enjoy visiting from the comfort of a front-held sling, which we're happy to loan.
Picnics in the courtyard are nice, and there's a children's menu in the restaurant.
We have a lift to help you get to other floors, and wheelchairs too.

Chirk Castle

Fortress   Garden   Parkland

Chirk Castle was built in the late 13th century and is a rather tough-looking character, with towers and thick brick walls, and a top-of-the-range dungeon on two levels. The castle stands on a hilltop looking over the Ceiriog valley to the south, so nobody can creep up on it unawares. The interior has been refurbished and added to over the years, and it's still home to the Myddleton family, whose ancestor Sir Thomas bought it in 1595 for a mere 5000 quid.

Bloody hand!

Legend has it that the red hand in the family coat-of-arms comes from a rather macabre running race. Two of the Myddleton lads argued over who should inherit, and agreed to settle the dispute by racing to the Castle gates. But the first boy was just reaching out to touch the gates when the other one reached out with his sword and cut off his hand. Now is that called cheating or 'winning on a technicality'?

What to see

- The rather grim dungeons with their very tiny windows. Don't get shut in!
- The 'murder holes' in the stairs in Adam's towers – soldiers threw hot oil and stones down them to hit the enemy below.
- Genuine suits of armour from the Civil War.
- The huge elaborate iron gates – look for the eagles' heads and the Myddelton family crest.

Chirk, Wrexham,
LL14 5AF. 01691 777701

OPENING TIMES

Castle
25 Mar–30 Jun 12pm–5pm
Wed–Sun
1 Jul–31 Aug 12pm–5pm
Tue–Sun
1 Sep–30 Sep 12pm–5pm
Wed–Sun
1 Oct–29 Oct 12pm–4pm
Wed–Sun

Garden, estate and farm
Dates as castle 10am–6pm
except Oct 10am–5pm

Restaurant
Dates as castle 10am–5pm
except Oct 10am–4pm

Shop
As for castle

Farm shop
25 Mar–30 Jun 10am–5pm
Wed–Sun
1 Jul–31 Aug 10am–6pm
Tue–Sun
1 Sep–30 Sep 10am–5pm
Wed–Sun
1 Oct–29 Oct 10pm–4pm
Wed–Sun

Notes
Open BH Mons.

Last admission
To garden 1hr before closing,
state rooms ½hr before closing

ADMISSION PRICES
£7, child £3.50, family £17.50.
Groups £5, child £2.50

Garden only
£4.50, child £2.20, family £11.20.
Groups £3.20, child £1.60

continued…

What to do

- Put the kids in the stocks (but please, do remember to take them home afterwards).
- Climb on the cannon.
- Have fun on the hanging ropes, tyres and wooden logs in the children's adventure playground.

Special events

We have family fun days when you can take part in lots of outdoor games and activities, and special themed days like our recent Haunted Happenings, and Jack the Jester circus workshops. The Sealed Knot also holds re-enactments of the Civil War. Usually there is no extra charge, but you may need to book for some things.

By the way...

- We have loads of touchable objects throughout the house, just ask.
- Wheelchairs are available and a stairlift. There are quite a few steps to get into the building and upper floors. The grounds are partly accessible.

Colby Woodland Garden

Here's a beautiful and peaceful garden in a secluded valley. Younger visitors will be wowed by the stunning displays of daffodils and bluebells in the Spring, and there are flowers all year round. Take a stroll down to the sea, or try one of the many other walks. Quizzes and activity packs make this a wonderful way to observe nature.

A glint of gold
If you think you see a glint of gold in the garden, you may be right. The gardens were formerly a mining valley. Anthracite – or 'black gold' – and iron ore were mined here until the end of the 19th century.

What to see
- A gothic gazebo in the gardens, with a strange painting inside it – have a peek through the window.
- Sculptures in the grounds.

What to do
- Take a gentle walk in the woods, or a longer trail – there are plenty of things to see (and seats!) along the way.
- Admire the local crafts displayed in the shop.
- Visit the walled garden (leave doggy friends outside, please).

By the way...
- Parts of the garden are very steep. Be careful – maybe not the best place for pushchairs or wheelchairs.
- Baby-changing facilities, and children's menu in the tea-room (not NT).

Amroth, Narberth,
Pembrokeshire, SA67 8PP
01834 811885

Wales & Northern Ireland

OPENING TIMES

**Woodland garden,
Shop/Gallery and tea-room**
26 Mar–29 Oct 10am–5pm
Daily

Walled garden
26 Mar–29 Oct 11am–5pm
Daily

ADMISSION PRICES
£4, child £2, family £10. Groups £3.40, child £1.70

Dinefwr Park

Historic house   Garden   Landscaped park   Walks

Llandeilo, Carmarthenshire, SA19 6RT. 01558 824512

OPENING TIMES

House
1 Jul–30 Oct 11am–5pm
Mon, Thur–Sun

Park
25 Mar–30 Oct 11am–5pm
Mon, Thur–Sun

Last admission
45 mins before closing

Notes
House opens in July after refurbishment; please telephone in advance if planning a visit in early July. Open daily during school hols.

ADMISSION PRICES
£5, child £2.50, family £12.50.
Groups £4.20

Park only
£3, child £1.50, family £7.50.
Groups £2.60

Dinefwr is a beautiful 18th-centry park enclosing a medieval deer park. Come into the house too, built in 1660 but now with a Victorian façade. Our friendly volunteers will be glad to tell you more, and little fingers are allowed to touch many of the objects. There are footpaths in the park leading to the castle, bog wood and some outstanding views of the Towy Valley.

The Romans woz 'ere
Recent geophys surveys show that there are not one but two big Roman forts hidden under the ground in Dinefwr Park. It could be the largest Roman garrison fort in Wales. Excavations began in June 2005 to find out just what's down there.

What to see
- Shy fallow deer munching away under the trees.
- A herd of rare Dinefwr White Park Cattle. They're very … white.
- A beautiful fancy ceiling in the house.

What to do
- Try out the children's house quiz; we'll help out if you get stuck!
- Enjoy a scenic walk: take the pushchair along our boardwalk through Bog Wood to the mill pond (see how many dragonflies you can spot there).
- Go on a park tour by tractor and trailer.

Special events
We often host family-friendly events. Recently we've had badger-watching and displays of vintage machines and classic cars. Give us a call to see what's on.

By the way...
- Dogs are allowed in the outer park only, on a lead.
- We have baby-changing and feeding facilities and a children's menu in the tea-room (not NT).
- You can book a wheelchair, and there's also a virtual tour of the house.

Dolaucothi Gold Mines

Mines Walks Museum

Come for a guided tour of the unique underground workings which have great archeological importance. And have a go at gold–panning. If you find any, it's yours. There's also an interesting new exhibition on mining history and working trains on the mine floor.

There's gold in them thar hills
… well, not much now, although the mines were in use from Roman times 2000 years ago, right up the 20th century. The Romans built a fort at Pumsaint, so they could keep an eye on things, and brought in slaves and local people to do the digging for them.

What to see
- Tunnels, pits, channels, tanks – basically, if you can dig one, it's probably here.
- A collection of 1930s mining machinery in the main mine yard.
- Pick marks in the rocks made by Roman slaves.

What to do
- Try gold-panning, and you'll realise just how frustrating looking for gold can be.
- Go for a walk in the wooded hills, or hire a cycle at the nearby Information Centre in Pumsaint.
- Experience what mining would have been like on the hour-long tour with only lamps to light your way (younger children allowed only at the discretion of staff – telephone to ask).

Special events
We have an annual living history weekend when we all go back to Roman times, and have visiting crafts and sometimes Roman cookery. You can come and join in – contact us to find out when this year's is.

By the way…
- We have a new level tour of the mine yard suitable for the less mobile.
- Good idea to wear good shoes for the underground tours; it can be a bit slippy down there.
- There's a caravan site and also fishing available on the estate.

Pumsaint, Llanwrda,
Carmarthenshire, SA19 8RR
01558 650177

OPENING TIMES
Mines
25 Mar–29 Oct 10am–5pm
Daily

Shop
25 Mar–29 Oct 10am–5pm
Daily

Christmas shop
8 Nov–17 Dec 11am–4pm
Wed–Sun

Tea-room
25 Mar–29 Oct 10am–5pm
Daily

Notes
Groups can be booked at other times. Pumsaint Information Centre and estate walks open all year.

ADMISSION PRICES
Site
£3.40, child £1.70, family £8.50.
Groups £3, child £1.50

Underground tour
(additional charge) £3.80, child £1.90, family £9.50. Groups £3.00, child £1.50
(NT members) £3.60, child £1.80, family £9.00

139

Erdigg

Historic house   Garden   Park   Woodland walks

Wrexham, LL13 0YT
01978 355314

OPENING TIMES
House
25 Mar–12 Apr 12pm–4pm
Mon–Wed, Sat, Sun
15 Apr–28 Jun 12pm–5pm
Mon–Wed, Sat, Sun
1 Jul–31 Aug 12pm–5pm
Mon–Thu, Sat, Sun
2 Sep–30 Sep 12pm–5pm
Mon–Wed, Sat, Sun
1 Oct–29 Oct 12pm–4pm
Mon–Wed, Sat, Sun

Garden
25 Mar–28 Jun 11am–6pm
Mon–Wed, Sat, Sun
1 Jul–31 Aug 10am–6pm
Mon–Thu, Sat, Sun
2 Sep–30 Sep 11am–6pm
Mon–Wed, Sat, Sun
1 Oct–29 Oct 11am–5pm
Mon–Wed, Sat, Sun
4 Nov–17 Dec 11–4pm Sat, Sun

Restaurant and shop/plants
25 Mar–28 Jun 11am–5.15pm
Mon–Wed, Sat, Sun
1 Jul–31 Aug 11am–5.15pm
Mon–Thu, Sat, Sun
2 Sep–30 Sep 11am–5.15pm
Mon–Wed, Sat, Sun
1 Oct–29 Oct 11am–4.15pm
Mon–Wed, Sat, Sun
4 Nov–17 Dec 11am–4pm
Sat, Sun

Notes
Open Good Fri

ADMISSION PRICES
£7.40, child £3.70, family £18.40.

Garden & outbuildings only
£3.80, child £1.90, family £9.20.

The original house was finished in 1687 and was added to over the years as the home of the Yorke family. They were a rather eccentric bunch and chose not to install electricity, gas or mains water until well into the 20th century. Don't be fooled by the plain brickwork exterior: inside, the lavish furnishing are outstanding and the servants' rooms give an intriguing taste of life 'below stairs'.

Family values
The Yorkes all shared an interest in antiquity and hoarding things, no matter how trivial. Many of them were vegetarians – in 1749 at age five, Philip Yorke apparently 'chused chiefly to dine on vegtables'. They were extremely fond of all their servants, and even commissioned portraits of them all – complete with little verses penned by the family.

What to see
- A grand kitchen – detached from the house to reduce the risk of fire. And many original objects in the stables, forge and more.
- An 18th-century waterfall known as the 'cup and saucer' in the park.
- Very special Chinese wallpaper in the house.

What to do

- Look for the gamekeeper, the housemaid and the blacksmith among the portraits of the servants in the servants' hall and basement passage.
- Visit the walled garden to spot rare breeds of fruit – did you know there was an apple called an Edlesborsdorfer? Neither did we!
- Take a horse-drawn carriage ride.

Special events

- We have authentic demonstrations of restored historic equipment, and sometimes you'll meet some 'Victorian' servants in the house. We also have special days, from kite-making to fancy dress. Call us to find out what holiday activities are planned.

By the way...

- We have wheelchairs, and a ramped entrance, but there are stairs in the house.
- Most rooms have no electric light – avoid dull days if you want a really close look at the pictures.
- There are three different walks to follow in the grounds, but please keep your dog on the lead.

Llanerchaeron

Historic house   Farm   Park   Garden

Ciliau Aeron, nr Aberaeron,
Ceredigion SA48 8DG
01545 570200

OPENING TIMES

House
25 Mar–23 Jul 11.30am-4.30pm
Wed–Sun
24 Jul–3 Sep 11.30am-4.30pm
Daily
6 Sep–29 Oct 11.30-4.30pm
Wed–Sun

Farm/garden
25 Mar–23 Jul 11am–5pm
Wed–Sun
24 Jul–3 Sep 11am–5pm
Daily
6 Sep–29 Oct 11am–5pm
Wed–Sun

Notes
Open BH Mons. Car park
closes at 5:30pm

ADMISSION PRICES
£6, child £3, family £15. Groups
£5, child £2.50. **Home Farm &
garden only:** £4.50, child
£2.10. Reduced rate when
arriving by cycle, on foot or by
public transport

Set in the beautiful Dyffryn Aeron, the estate survived virtually
unaltered into the 20th century.

Do It Yourself
No trips to the supermarket here, everything consumed or used on the
property was produced here – the house is an great example of self-
sufficiency. The workers would have produced all their own cheese and
milk in the Dairy, they'd have salted their own meats for preservation
and even brewed their own beer!

What to see
- Visit the dairy, laundry, brewery and salting house and learn how
  they would have made everything themselves.
- The restored walled gardens full of home-grown fruit, vegetables
  and herbs.
- Traditional farming activities in progress: lambing, shearing and
  hay-making.

What to do
- Home Farm is a working organic farm, so there's loads to learn
  about, take a guided tour and then visit the Education Centre.
- Enjoy one of the many walks around the estate and parkland.
- Learn about the breeds of animals, including Welsh Black Cattle,
  Llanwenog Sheep and rare Welsh pigs.

By the way...
- Parents can take part in Adult Study days.

Penrhyn Castle

Castle   Adventure playground   Museums   Park   Woodland

Penrhyn looks like a fairytale medieval castle, but actually it was built in the 19th century. So, who cares if it's a fake – it's well worth a visit because it's packed with goodies, like the doll's museum and railway museum, and has a wonderful adventure playground too.

Easy as A B C
Richard Pennant, who lived here, made a fortune from the local slate quarry. Every year his workers made 136,000 slates for children to write on in school. Wonder if the children were grateful!

What to see
- An industrial railway museum in the stable block, and a model railway museum.
- A large collection of 19th- and 20th-century dolls.
- And can you spot two chamber pots in the dining room? They were there so the men didn't have to leave to go to the loo after dinner – yuck!

What to do
- Visit the Victorian servants' quarters, set up to show the preparations for the banquet put on for the Prince of Wale in 1894. They had pineapple ice cream and foie gras in aspic. Very tasty.
- Look at the one-ton slate bed made for Queen Victoria. Sounds pretty uncomfortable.
- Explore the formal Victorian walled garden and the adventure playground.

Bangor, Gwynedd,
LL57 4HN.
01248 353084

OPENING TIMES

Castle
25 Mar–30 Jun 12pm–5pm
Mon, Wed–Sun
1 Jul–31 Aug 11am–5pm
Mon, Wed–Sun
1 Sep–29 Oct 12pm–5pm
Mon, Wed–Sun

Grounds, tea-room
25 Mar–30 Jun 11am–5pm
Mon, Wed–Sun
1 Jul–31 Aug 10am–5pm
Mon, Wed–Sun
1 Sep–29 Oct 11am–5pm
Mon, Wed–Sun

Shop
25 Mar–29 Oct 11am–5pm
Mon, Wed–Sun

Museums
25 Mar–29 Oct 11am–5pm
Mon, Wed–Sun

Last admission
Castle and grounds: last admission 4.30pm
Victorian kitchen: as castle but last admission 4.45pm. Last audio tour 4pm

ADMISSION PRICES
£8, child £4, family £20.
Groups £6.50

Garden and stable block exhibitions only
£5.40, child £2.70

continued…   143

Special events
We have quite a few family events and activitie. Recently we've had Knights and Castles Fun Day, archery and hands-on cooking activities. Call us to find out what's planned.

By the way...
- Baby-changing and feeding facilities, plus sling loan (sorry, no pushchairs in the house). Children's guide and quiz/trail and also a children's menu.
- Touchable objects, including engines in the Railway Museum.
- We can lend you a wheelchair, and the entrance is ramped. There are stairs to the upper floors.

Plas Newydd

Historic house　Boat trip　Garden　Museum　Walks

A very grand ivy-covered mansion, Plas Newydd simply means 'new place' in Welsh. It was built in the 18th century, and is still home to the Marquess of Anglesey. There's a big collection of paintings by Rex Whistler and a Military museum with interesting artifacts. It is set in large gardens, with a marine walk along the Menai Straits and spectacular views of Snowdonia.

Like our new place?

The Plas was home to Lady Eleanor Butler and the Honourable Sarah Ponsoby, known to the locals as the Ladies of Llangollen. They did their new place up with sumptuous gardens, a circular stone dairy and servants and invited Wordsworth, Shelley and Byron along. Then they found they'd got a wee bit into debt.

Llanfairpwll, Anglesey,
LL61 6DQ. 01248 714795

OPENING TIMES
House
1 Apr–1 Nov 12pm–5pm
Mon–Wed, Sat, Sun

Garden
1 Apr–1 Nov 11am–5.30pm
Mon–Wed, Sat, Sun

Walks
As for garden

Shop
1 Apr–1 Nov 10.30am–5.30pm
Mon-Wed, Sat, Sun.
4 Nov–17 Dec 11am–4pm
Sat, Sun

Tea-room
As for shop

Notes
Open Good Fri. Rhododendron garden open 1 Apr–early Jun, 11am–5.30pm

ADMISSION PRICES
£6, child £3, family £15. Groups £5.40

Garden only
£4.00, child £2

Wales & Northern Ireland

continued…

What to see

- An enormous painting by Rex Whistler – can you find Neptune's footsteps?
- An artificial leg made for the 1st Marquess of Anglesey. Her father carelessly lost the real one in the Battle of Waterloo.
- A circle of stones in the garden, used for an Eisteddfod (a traditional Welsh singing and poetry competition) in 1908.

What to do

- Have a go at the children's quiz trail that leads you through the grounds.
- Clamber in the tree house, built for the Marquess's kids.
- For an additional charge, you can take an historical boat trip that departs from the house; it takes around 40 minutes.

Special events

We've had spooky Halloween fun days, circus workshops, and jazz nights in the past. Contact us to see what's on.

By the way...

- It's licensed for civil weddings, if you'd like a nice Plas to get hitched in.
- Family friendly with baby-changing facilities and baby slings for loans, as well as a children's play area.
- Lower floors accessible, and there are wheelchairs available.

Powis Castle & Gardens

Historic house   Garden   Museum

If you like the idea of a dramatic medieval castle rising over world-famous gardens with statues and even an aviary, Powis is for you. The castle was originally built around 1200, as a fortress for the Welsh Princes of Powys. Over the years the Herbert family have packed it with paintings, sculptures and a fascinating collection of treasures from India, displayed in the Clive Museum.

What's in a name, Clive?

Edward Clive (1785–1848) inherited Powis from his uncle, but only if he agreed to change his name to Herbert. Things didn't end so well – he was shot to death by one of his own sons in a tragic accident. This son was apparently known to other members of the family ever after as 'Bag Dad' – not in the best of taste!

What to see

- A solid gold tiger head encrusted with precious stones.
- 300-year-old giant yew hedges – imagine clipping those without electric clippers.
- The igloo shaped ice house – used to store ice before fridges came along.

What to do

- Have a go at the children's quiz.
- Find a giant stone foot sculpture in the Wilderness Garden.
- Run up and down the steep garden terraces.

Special events

Our intrepid hedging team explains how they look after those yews, and at other times you can have a behind-the-scenes look at the private rooms and museum. There are some holiday activities and an annual Easter Egg hunt. Get in touch for more information.

By the way...

- Powis is very popular and we have timed tickets at busy periods.
- Because of the steep gardens and steps, it's not very accessible to people in wheelchairs.

Welshpool, Powys,
SY21 8RF. 01938 551944

OPENING TIMES

Castle/museum
6 Apr–30 Jun 1pm–5pm
Mon, Thu–Sun
1 Jul–31 Aug 1pm–5pm
Mon, Wed–Sun
1 Sep–17 Sep 1pm–5pm
Mon, Thur–Sun
18 Sep–29 Oct 1pm–4pm
Mon, Thur–Sun

Garden
25 Mar–2 Apr 11am–5pm
Sat, Sun
6 Apr–30 Jun 11am–6pm
Mon, Thur–Sun
1 Jul–31 Aug 11am–6pm
Mon, Wed–Sun
1 Sep–17 Sep 11am–6pm
Mon, Thu–Sun
18 Sep–29 Oct 11am–5pm
Mon, Thu–Sun

Coach house
6 Apr–30 Jun 11am–4.30pm
Mon, Thu–Sun
1 Jul–31 Aug 11am–4.30pm
Mon, Wed–Sun
1 Sep–29 Oct 11am–4.30pm
Mon, Thu–Sun

Restaurant/shop
Please see National Trust website for details.

Last admission
45 mins before closing.

ADMISSION PRICES
£9.60, child £4.80, family £24.
Groups £8.60

Garden only
£6.60, child £3.30, family £16.
Groups £5.60

CASTLES & CHIVALRY

Castles and other defensive buildings were built to keep unwanted visitors out, whether they came by sea or land. The National Trust looks after many castles and other fortified buildings that we'd love you to visit – come and explore!

Castles on the coast

Britain has always needed fortifications to protect itself against invaders, from the 14th-century **Dunstanburgh Castle** in Northumberland to the Victorian defences at the **Needles Old Battery**. While Dunstanburgh is a real fairy tale castle, rising out of the mist on a foggy day, **Lindisfarne Castle** is a wonderful mix of Tudor architecture, a Romantic island separated from the mainland by a causeway, and a very special interior designed by Lutyens.

Inland defences

Rayleigh Mount in Essex is an 11th-century 'motte and bailey' castle, one of the earliest still in evidence. The motte, or moat, was enthusiastically used in medieval castles like the impressive **Bodiam** in East Sussex, one of the most 'castle-y' castles we've ever seen. Then there's **Chirk Castle** in Wrexham, rising over the Welsh Marches with a view over five counties, and **Tattershall Castle** in Lincolnshire, with six floors of goodies to explore.

Moats also turn up in fancy manor houses like 15th-century **Oxburgh Hall**, **Ightham Mote** in Kent and, a little later, Speke Hall near Liverpool. Before the days of CCTV and alarms, a moat was a pretty good deterrent. And many places also had 'murder holes' to pour boiling oil or water on the unsuspecting enemy below. Not very nice!

Sizergh Castle in Cumbria may really be a large Elizabethan house, but it certainly looks like a castle. And then there's **Greys Court** in Oxfordshire, an intriguing Tudor Manor with 14th-century fortifications. Mary Queen of Scots was imprisoned here under the orders of Elizabeth 1.

Keeping out the nasty neighbours was sometimes a real problem. At least being up on a hill gave you a chance to see 'em coming, and **Powis Castle** in Wales is well worth the climb because the 18th-century gardens are fantastic. The 1000-year-old **Corfe Castle** has been a stronghold in Dorset since the time of William the Conquerer, and is now a majestic ruin with wonderful grounds. **Dunster Castle** in Somerset also has an ancient history, although the present building is 19th-century, and the gardens are palatial, too.

Fairytale castles?

Perhaps we'd all like to make our home our castle. And throughout the ages some of the more wealthy have done that. Some castles are just there for the fun of it – and we're sure you'll enjoy the fun of investigating the imaginative nooks and crannies

of **Penrhyn Castle** in Bangor, Wales. Built in the 19th century and complete with neo-Norman fancy towers, crenellated ramparts and loads of impressive walls, it's a real fantasy castle. It does also have a fully equipped Victorian kitchen and a model railway museum, though. Then there's **Castle Drogo**, sometimes called 'the last castle to be built in England'. It certainly looks spectacular, but it's another Lutyens confection that isn't a real castle, and was built for a millionaire whose name wasn't really Drogo. Well, who's arguing?

And just to finish up, how many windows do you think there are at Alport Castles? None, it's a trick question! **Alport Castles** are a spectacular landscape feature in the Peak District, formed by a massive land-slip. Even so, they're still well worth a look!

Visit the National Trust website at **www.nationaltrust.org.uk** to find more information about the many other castles and defensive buildings owned by the National Trust.

The Argory

Historic house   Adventure playground   Sculpture trail

Wales & Northern Ireland

144 Derrycaw Road, Moy,
Dungannon, Co. Armagh,
BT71 6NA. 028 8778 4753

OPENING TIMES

House
18 Mar–9 Apr 1pm–6pm
Sat, Sun
14 Apr–23 Apr 1pm–6pm Daily
29 Apr–28 May 1pm–6pm
Sat, Sun
1 Jun–31 Aug 1pm–6pm Daily
2 Sep–30 Sep 1pm–6pm
Sat, Sun

Shop
As for house 1pm–5:30pm

Tea-room
As for house 2pm–5.30pm

Grounds
1 May–30 Sep 10am–7pm Daily
1 Oct–30 Apr 10am–4pm Daily

Notes
Admission by guided tour.
Open BH Mons and all other
public hols in N Ireland inc. 17
Mar. Please note, house and
grounds open at 2pm on
special event days.

ADMISSION PRICES
£4.70, child £2.50, family
£11.90. Groups £4.20

A very imposing house from the 1820s, with lovely garden and woodlands and beautiful riverside walks. It's a real time capsule: not much has changed since 1900, when the Bond family lived there.

Oh do clear up!

The Bond's family treasures include a weighing chair, books, portraits, clothing and a rather large working barrel organ, which is still played for our 'musical house tours'. Next time you're told to tidy your room, try explaining that you're starting a museum!

What to see
- Horse carriages, a harness room and a laundry.
- The acetylene gas plant (hint, they don't need watering…) in the stableyard.
- A sundial in the middle of the rose garden.

What to do
- Explore the playground and the environmental sculpture trail.
- Visit the award-winning Lady Ada's tea-room – our cakes are second to none!
- Avoid dull days if you want a really good look – there's no electric light (honestly, these Edwardians…).

Special events
There's an exciting programme of events all year, including our Victorian Christmas Fayre, when you enjoy music, festive food (and a visit from Santa, too!).

By the way…
- Try the children's quiz trail. Changing facilities, and baby slings for hire.
- The ground floor's accessible, and we have 2 wheelchairs.

Castle Ward & Strangford Lough

Historic house   Playgrounds   Victorian pastime   Wildlife centres

Here's a house that can't make up its mind – one façade is Classical and the other side is Gothic. In fact, Castle Ward is famous for its mix of architectural styles, inside and out, as well as the breathtaking views across Strangford Lough. Worth a visit in spring especially, for acres of bluebells.

Strangford Lough

From Castle Ward you can watch huge flocks of Pale-bellied Brent Geese coming south over this huge seawater lake. There's a festival every autumn to celebrate their arrival. There are also seals and otters. The name means 'strong fjord', and the current is indeed very strong – look out for sailboats going backwards, or the ferry struggling against the current.

What to see

- Farm animals – including rare Irish moiled cattle; moiled means 'hornless'.
- Farm machinery in the farmyard.
- The basement and tunnel inside the house.
- See – and touch – all the interesting natural objects in the Wildlife Centre.

Strangford, Downpatrick, Co. Down, BT30 7LS
028 4488 1204

OPENING TIMES

House & wildlife centre
1 Apr–13 Apr 1pm–6pm Sat, Sun
14 Apr–23 Apr 1pm–6pm Daily
1 Jul–31 Aug 1pm–6pm Daily
2 Sep–30 Aug 1pm–6pm Sat, Sun

Grounds
1 May–30 Sep 10am–8pm Daily
1 Oct–30 Apr 10am–4pm Daily

Tea room & shop
As for house 1pm–5.30pm

Notes

Admission by guided tour. Open BH Mons and all other public holidays in N Ireland inc. 17 Mar. Last house tour starts at 5pm. Commill operations Sun during open season

ADMISSION PRICES

House, grounds & wildlife centre
£5.50, child £2.50, family £13.50. Groups £4.60

Grounds & wildlife centre only:
£3.80, child £1.80, family £9.40. Groups £3.20

continued…

151

What to do
- There's a playground for under-10s as well as a spectacular adventure playground for those with longer legs.
- For a small extra charge, take a ride around the grounds on the Castle Ward Cruise – a tractor towed trailer.
- Dress up and play with period toys in the Victorian Past Times Centre.
- Take a picnic or food for a barbecue, and play ball games on the lawns.

Special events
Recent events include nature rambles, craft fayres and a teddy bears' picnic. Or you might go on a bat walk or a moth morning. Contact us to find out what we have planned.

By the way...
- There are many steps at the front; an alternative entrance has fewer. Wheelchairs can be booked.
- Baby-changing facilities and hip-carry seats for loan. There's a children's menu in the tea-room too.

Crom Estate

Woods   Park   Wetland   Boat hire   Walks

If you fancy a spot of fishing, camping or would like to hire a boat to splosh around in a magical maze of water, peninsulas and islands, then Crom's your place. Set on the shores of Upper Lough Erne, this area is rightfully one of the Trust's most important nature reserves.

Wild about life
There are many rare species here, including pine martens, red squirrels and badgers. Put on good shoes and get back to nature. Or put on your best togs and get married – we're licensed for civil weddings, too.

What to see
- Wild garlic (pretty, not pong-y), violets and rare mosses and lichens.
- The purple hair streak butterfly – what a name!
- Cormorants and curlews – listen out for the curlew's shrill cry.

What to do
- Arrange to stay overnight in the mammal hide to look out for pine martens.
- Wend your way around the islands in a hired boat, or ride through the reserve on the Kingfisher Trail cycle path.
- Explore one of the trails, or take a guided tour.

Special events
We have some summer events like small pet competitions and garden fairs; get in touch for more details. And don't forget – you can stay in our camp site, too.

By the way...
- Dogs on lead only, please, but welcome.
- The 19th-century castle you'll see is not open to the public. But our award-winning Visitor Centre and tea-room is, so do pop in.
- You can book our wheelchair, and the grounds have an accessible route.

Upper Lough Erne, Newtownbutler, Co. Fermanagh, BT92 8AP. 028 6773 8118

OPENING TIMES
Grounds
11 Mar–30 Jun 10am–6pm Daily
1 Jul–31 Aug 10am–7pm Daily
1 Sep–30 Sep 10am–6pm Daily
1 Oct–15 Oct 12pm–6pm
Sat, Sun

Visitor Centre
11 Mar–13 Apr 10am–6pm
Sat, Sun
14 Apr–23 Apr 10am–6pm Daily
24 Apr–30 Apr 10am–6pm
Sat, Sun
1 May–30 Sep 10am–6pm Daily

Notes
Open BH Mons and all other public holidays in N Ireland inc. 17 Mar. Every Sun grounds and visitor centre open 12pm–6pm. Tel. property for shop and tea-room opening arrangements

ADMISSION PRICES
Grounds & visitor centre
Car or boat £4.80, minibus £13.50, coach £17, motorbike £2

Campsite charge
£10 per tent per night

Florence Court

Historic house   Playground   Park   Walks

Enniskillen, Co. Fermanagh,
BT92 1DB. 028 6634 8249

OPENING TIMES

House
17 Mar–19 Mar 1pm–6pm
Fri–Sun
1 Apr–13 Apr 1pm–6pm
Sat, Sun
14 Apr–23 Apr 1pm–6pm Daily
24 Apr–28 May 1pm–6pm
Sat, Sun
1 Jun–30 Jun 1pm–6pm
Mon, Wed–Sun
1 Jul–31 Aug 12pm–6pm Daily
2 Sep–30 Sep 1pm–6pm
Sat, Sun

Grounds
1 Apr–29 Oct 10am–8pm Daily
30 Oct–31 Mar 10am–4pm
Daily

Notes
Admission by guided tour to
house. Open BH Mons and all
other public holidays in N
Ireland inc. 17 Mar. Last
admission 1hr before closing.

ADMISSION PRICES

House tour
£4.25, child £2, family £10.50.
Groups £3.50

Grounds
Car £3, minibus £15, coach £20

One of Ulster's most important 18th-century houses, which used to
be home to the Earls of Enniskillen. The setting is lovely, with the
Cuilcagh mountains as a dramatic backdrop to the grounds, and a
mill and a walled garden to explore. There's also a playground for
smaller people's adventures.

That's a bit fishy...
William Willoughby Cole, 3rd earl of Enniskillen (1807–1886) was a
palaeontologist – he studied ancient rocks and fossils. He was
particularly keen on collecting fossil fishes. Now they're in the Natural
History Museum in London, although there are lots of other oddities in
the house.

What to see
- The famous Florence Court Yew tree, supposed to be the 'parent' of
  all Irish yew trees.
- A hydraulic ram and water-powered saw-mill in the grounds.
- A blacksmith's forge, carpenter's workshop and an eel house. And
  an ice-house, from the days before fridges kept things cool.

What to do
- On Sundays in summer, go on one of our 'Living History Tours' to
  get a taste of life in the house.
- Swing and snack in the playground and picnic area.
- Try out the quiz and trail for younger members.

Special events
Summer weekends are a good time to find special family activities like
children's fun days, craft shows and even Victorian fashion shows. And
we have a spooky Halloween Craft Fayre with face-painting – and
perhaps ghosts! Give us a call.

By the way...
- We have wheelchairs, and a ramp is available. The 1400-metre
  (¾-mile) path around the grounds is mostly very suitable for
  pushchairs or wheelchairs.
- Baby-changing and baby slings for loan.
- Dogs on the lead, please.

Giant's Causeway
Rock formations   Walks

These rock formations really do look as if they were made for giants to stroll along. Discovered by the Bishop of Derry, in the 1600s, they have amazed visitors ever since. There are lovely paths to follow along the coastline, and the area is both an Area of Outstanding Natural Beauty and the only World Heritage Site in Northern Ireland.

Fee foe fie Finn
Legend has it the causeway was built by giant Finn McCool so he could walk to Scotland and fight Benandonner. Finn fell asleep on the way, and his clever wife put a blanket over him. When Benandonner came along she pretended Finn was her baby. Benandonner figured if that's the baby, his Dad must be pretty darned big, and ran off home! Actually the 40,000-odd basalt columns are the result of volcanic eruptions, over 60 million years ago. But even that is pretty amazing.

What to see
- Hexagonal (six-sided) stepping stones in the causeway. But can you see some that have five, seven or even eight sides?
- A video history of the Causeway.
- Lots of seabirds and other wildlife from the cliffs (but don't get too near the edge!)

What to do
- Follow the North Antrim Coastal path and read the info panels.
- If you walk far enough, you'll get to the Carrik-a-Rede rope bridge.
- Sit in the Wishing Chair rock and make a wish.

By the way...
- There's a ramped entrance to the visitor centre, and a wheelchair available. We can provide a map of an accessible route.
- It's a good idea to wear good shoes if you're going to have a walk.
- Dogs on leads are welcome, as are pushchairs and baby carriers. Tea room, children's menu and baby-changing facilities.

c/o 44a Causeway Road,
Bushmills, Co. Antrim,
BT57 8SU. 028 2073 1582

OPENING TIMES
The stones and coast are open all year round. except 25 Dec and 26 Dec

Notes
Tel. for shop and tea-room opening times

ADMISSION PRICES
Admission free. Donations welcome. Group guided tours £3, child £2

Mount Stewart House

Garden   Temple of the Winds   Historic house   Walks

Wales & Northern Ireland

Portaferry Road, Newtownards,
Co. Down, BT22 2AD
028 4278 8387

OPENING TIMES

Lakeside Gardens
1 Apr–30 Apr 10am–6pm Daily
1 May–30 Sep 10am–8pm Daily
1 Oct–31 Oct 10am–6pm Daily
1 Nov–31 Mar 10am–4pm Daily

Formal Gardens
11 Mar–26 Mar 10am–4pm
Sat, Sun
1 Apr–30 Apr 10am–6pm Daily
1 May–30 Sep 10am–8pm Daily
1 Oct–31 Oct 10am–6pm Daily

House
11 Mar–13 Apr 12pm–6pm
Sat, Sun
14 Apr–23 Apr 12pm–6pm Daily
24 Apr–30 Apr 12pm–6pm
Sat, Sun
1 May–31 May 1pm–6pm
Mon, Wed–Sun
1 Jun–30 Jun 1pm–6pm Daily
1 Jul–31 Aug 12pm–6pm Daily
1 Sep–30 Sep 1pm–6pm
Mon, Wed–Sun
1 Oct–29 Oct 12pm–6pm
Sat, Sun

Temple
2 Apr–24 Sep 2pm–5pm Sun

Notes
Open BH Mons and public
holidays, inc. 17 Mar. Tel. or see
website for shop and restaurant
hours

ADMISSION PRICES

House & gardens
£5.50, child £2.80, family
£13.80. Groups £5

Gardens only
£4.50, child £2.40, family £11.40.
Groups £4

The famous gardens here are among the best in the care of the National Trust, laid out in the 1920s by Lady Londonderry in a series of different garden rooms, or 'parterres'. There's something new around every corner, and many dramatic views. The house has world-famous paintings, including a very famous painting of a horse by George Stubbs, almost large as life. The socialite Londonderry family were great party-givers, and entertained many well-known politicians, including Winston Churchill. Storys and mementoes abound in the house.

Animal magic

Lady Londonderry made all the politicians who visited members of her elite Ark Club. You can see animal pictures of them in the tearoom – Winston Churchill was 'Winnie the Warlock'. Wonder which animal today's prime minister would be?

What to see

- Dinosaurs In the garden, and a horse with a monkey on its back.
- Find 'Mairi Mairi quite contrary' sitting in the middle of a pond – with her cockle shells, of course.
- Real banana trees.

What to do

- Creep down the underground tunnel by the Temple of Wind.
- Find the crocodile and the dodo in the gardens.
- Picnic by the main gates and enjoy the view over Strangford Lough.

Special events

We have summer jazz concerts that all the family can enjoy, on the last Sunday of the month from April to September. Activities for smaller visitors include Dinosaur Day and Santa's Grotto. Get in touch to find what's on and book if necessary.

By the way...

- The entrance to the property is level and we have wheelchairs available, though you need to book.
- There's a special sensory trail in the gardens; ask for details at reception.
- We have baby-changing facilities and a children's menu in the restaurant.

Springhill & Wellbrook

Historic house   Museum   Play area   Walks   Mill

Wellbrook offers some lovely walks and picnic places by the Ballinderry River. The mill has its original hammer machinery, and demonstrations of the linen process by costumed guides. Down the road Springhill is an atmospheric house with an unusual and colourful costume exhibition.

No beetles were harmed in the making of this... Beetling is actually the final stage in the production of linen, a very important industry in 19th-century Ireland. Hammer machinery was used to beat a sheen into the cloth. No beetles involved!

What to see
- At Springhill, Kentucky rifles and blunderbusses.
- A nursery packed with toys, and the excellent costume museum.
- At Wellbrook, 30 massive noisy hammers working the linen (ear plugs, please!).

What to do
- At Springhill, try on copies of clothes from long ago in the children's centre.
- Or visit the shell house and the play area.
- At Wellbrook, have a go at beetling, and try out the spinning wheel – it's much harder than you think!

By the way...
- At Springhill and Wellbrook, pushchairs and back-carriers are ok, and dogs on leads are welcome in the grounds.
- If steps are a problem, ask to use the alternative entrance at Springhill. We can lend a wheelchair at Springhill.
- There's a handling collection at Wellbrook, and a guide available to talk to visitors. There are some steps involved in the house.

Springhill
20 Springhill Road, Moneymore, Magherafelt, Co. Londonderry, BT45 7NQ   028 8674 8210

Wellbrook Beetling Mill
20 Wellbrook Road, Corkhill, Cookstown, Co. Tyrone, BT80 9RY.   028 8674 8210

OPENING TIMES
Springhill
1 Apr–13 Apr 1pm–6pm
Sat, Sun
14 Apr–23 Apr 1pm–6pm Daily
24 Apr–25 Jun 1pm–6pm
Sat, Sun
1 Jul–31 Aug 1pm–6pm Daily
2 Sep–30 Sep 1pm–6pm
Sat, Sun

Mill
1 Apr–13 Apr 1pm–6pm
Sat, Sun
14 Apr–23 Apr, 1pm–6pm Daily
24 Apr–25 Jun 1pm–6pm
Sat, Sun
1 Jul–31 Aug 1pm–6pm Daily
2 Sep–30 Sep 1pm–6pm
Sat, Sun

Notes
Admission by guided tour. Open BH Mons and public holidays, inc. 17 Mar. Last admission 1hr before closing. Tel property for shop opening times.

ADMISSION PRICES
Springhill
£4.30, child £2.30, family £10.90. Groups £3.70

Mill
£3.10, child £1.80, family £8. Groups £2.60

Index

Photographic credits

Front Cover NTPL/Jennie Woodcock; Back Cover (left) NTPL/Ian Shaw; Back Cover (centre): NTPL/Ian Shaw; Back Cover (right): NTPL/Andrew Butler; Spine (top) NTPL/Ian Shaw; Spine (bottom): Dudmaston NTPL/David Levenson; page 1 NTPL/Jennie Woodcock; 2 NTPL/Stephen Robson; 6 NTPL/Ian Shaw; 7 NTPL/Jennie Woodcock; 8 NTPL/Michael Caldwell; 9 NTPL/David Levenson; 11 NTPL/Ian Shaw; 12 NTPL/Jennie Woodcock; 15 NTPL/Matthew Antrobus; 16 NTPL/David Noton; 17 NTPL/Joe Cornish; 18 NTPL/Joe Cornish; 19 NTPL/Andrew Butler; 20 NTPL/Andrew Butler; 21 NTPL/Chris Gascoigne; 22 NTPL/David Levenson; 23 NTPL/Matthew Antrobus; 24 NTPL/David Noton; 25 NTPL/Nadia Mackenzie; 26 (top) NTPL/Ian Shaw; 26 (bottom) NTPL; 27 (top) NTPL/John Miller; 27(bottom) NTPL/Geraint Tellem; 28 NTPL/Ian Shaw; 29 NTPL/Stephen Robson; 30 NTPL/Andrew Butler; 31 NTPL/Andreas von Einsiedel; 32 NTPL/Jerry Harpur; 33 NTPL/Andreas von Einsiedel; 34 NTPL/Derek Croucher; 35 NTPL/Nigel Hicks; 37 NTPL/Derek Croucher; 38 NTPL/Andrea Jones; 39 NTPL/Derek Croucher; 40 NTPL/Geoffrey Frosh; 41 NTPL/Geoffrey Frosh; 42 NTPL/Andrew Butler; 44 NTPL/Andrew Butler; 45 NTPL/Derek Croucher; 47 NTPL/Ian Shaw; 48 (top) NTPL/Paul Wakefield; 48 (bottom) NTPL/Ian Shaw; 49 (top) NTPL/Joe Cornish; 49 (bottom) NTPL/NaturePL/Hans Christoph Kappel; 50 NTPL/Leo Mason; 51 NTPL/Jennie Woodcock; 52 NTPL/Derek Croucher; 53 NTPL/Andy Williams; 54 NTPL/Ian West; 55 NTPL/Andreas von Einsiedel; 56 NTPL/Ian Shaw; 57 NTPL/Stephen Robson; 58 NTPL/Ian West; 59 NTPL/Ian Shaw; 60 NTPL/Stephen Robson; 61 NTPL/Jennie Woodcock; 62 NTPL/Rupert Truman; 63 NTPL/Bill Batten; 64 NTPL/Chris King; 65 NTPL/Ian Shaw; 66 NTPL/Ian Shaw; 67 NTPL/David Levenson; 68 NTPL/Angelo Hornak; 70 NTPL/Paul Wakefield; 71 NTPL/Paul Wakefield; 72 NTPL/Rod J.Edwards; 73 NTPL/Andreas von Einsiedel; 74 NTPL/Rupert Truman; 75 NTPL/Matthew Antrobus; 77 NTPL/Mike Williams; 78 NTPL/Andrew Butler; 79 NTPL/David Levenson; 80 NTPL/Ian Shaw; 81 (top) NTPL/Charlie Waite; 81 (bottom) NTPL/Ian Shaw; 82 NTPL/Ian Shaw; 83 NTPL/Jennie Woodcock; 84 NTPL/Andreas von Einsiedel; 85 NTPL/Andrew Butler; 86 NTPL/Ian Shaw; 87 NTPL/Paul Harris; 88 NTPL/Andreas von Einsiedel; 89 NTPL/Andreas von Einsiedel; 90 NTPL/Michael Caldwell; 91 NTPL/David Levenson; 92 NTPL/Ian Shaw; 93 NTPL/David Levenson; 94 NTPL/Nick Meers; 95 NTPL/Andrew Haslam; 96 NTPL/Andreas von Einsiedel; 97 NTPL/Andreas von Einsiedel; 98 NTPL/Ian Shaw; 99 NTPL/Ian Shaw; 100 NTPL/Nick Meers; 101 NTPL/Andreas von Einsiedel; 102 NTPL/Chris King; 103 NTPL/Dennis Gilbert; 104 NTPL/Andrew Butler; 105 NTPL/Stephen Robson; 106 NTPL/Geoffrey Frosh; 107 NTPL/Nick Meers; 108 NTPL/Joe Cornish; 109 NTPL/Joe Cornish; 110 NTPL/Rupert Truman; 111 NTPL/Matthew Antrobus; 112 (top) NTPL/Joe Cornish; 112 (bottom) NTPL/Joe Cornish; 113 (top) NTPL/Leo Mason; 113 (bottom) NTPL/Joe Cornish; 114 NTPL/Dennis Gilbert; 115 NTPL/Mike Williams; 116 NTPL/Rupert Truman; 117 NTPL/J.Whitaker; 118 NTPL/Joe Cornish; 119 NTPL/John Hammond; 120 NTPL/Matthew Antrobus; 121 NTPL/Andrew Butler; 123 NTPL/David Levenson; 124 NTPL/Lee Frost; 125 NTPL/Paul Wakefield; 126 NTPL/Stephen Robson; 127 NTPL/Stephen Robson; 128 NTPL/Joe Cornish; 129 NTPL/Joe Cornish; 130 NTPL/Andreas von Einsiedel; 131 NTPL/Mike Williams; 132 NTPL/Matthew Antrobus; 133 NTPL/Will Curwen; 134 NTPL/Matthew Antrobus; 135 NTPL/Andreas von Einsiedel; 136 NTPL/Matthew Antrobus; 137 NTPL/Andrew Butler; 138 NTPL/Andrew Butler; 139 NTPL/Andrew Butler; 140 NTPL/John Hammond; 141 NTPL/Andreas von Einsiedel; 142 NTPL/Ian Shaw; 143 NTPL/Michael Caldwell; 144 NTPL/Michael Caldwell; 145 NTPL; 146 NTPL/Nick Meers; 147 NTPL/Ian Shaw; 148 (top) NTPL/David Dixon; 148 (bottom) NTPL/Alasdair Ogilvie; 149 NTPL/Andrew Butler; 150 NTPL/Andreas von Einsiedel; 151 NTPL/Ian Shaw; 152 NTPL/Joe Cornish; 153 NTPL/Joe Cornish; 154 NTPL/Derek Croucher; 155 NTPL/Joe Cornish;156 NTPL/Ian Shaw; 157 NTPL/Andreas von Einsiedel

National Trust membership

Whether you're interested in gardens, castles, wildlife, places linked to famous events or people, you're looking for a new coastal path to walk or just somewhere peaceful to relax and enjoy a nice cup of tea, National Trust membership gives you a wide variety of things to do, as often as you like, for free.

Join today and you can start to explore some of Britain's most beautiful places, while helping to protect them for future generations.

As a member you'll receive a comprehensive membership pack featuring places cared for by the National Trust.

What's more, National Trust membership gives you free entry to more than 300 historic houses and gardens and information about 700 miles of coastline and almost 250,000 hectares of stunning countryside, so visiting couldn't be easier.

Visit www.nationaltrust.org.uk or phone 0870 458 4000 for more details.